SIX GENERATIONS

SIX GENERATIONS
Life and work in Ireland from 1790

based on the RTE series
by L. M. Cullen

Published in association with
Radio Telefís Éireann
by
THE MERCIER PRESS
CORK and DUBLIN

The Mercier Press, 4 Bridge Street, Cork
24 Lower Abbey Street, Dublin 1.

© Radio Telefís Éireann 1970

ISBN 0 85342 227 3

First published 1970
This edition 1986

CONTENTS

The series, *Six Generations*, was produced for television by Radio
Telefís Éireann, in association with the Department of Education.
Dr. L. M. Cullen's original scripts were adapted for television by
Brendan Scott and Jack White, and were edited for publication
by Jack White. Research on illustrations by Póilín ní Chiaráin.

An Irish farmer of the 18th century: from a print by Hincks in the Ulster Museum.

Preface

This book is about the way people lived and worked in Ireland during the last six generations. At the usual reckoning of about 30 years to a generation, this takes us back 180 years: roughly from the time of Grattan's Parliament to the present day.

The great political events of that period were the Act of Union in 1800, by which Ireland lost her Parliament; Catholic Emancipation in 1829; the Great Famine; the Young Ireland movement; the Fenian rising; the rise of the Land League and Parnell; the campaign for Home Rule; and finally the resurgence of this century—the 1916 Rising and the War of Independence.

These are the events that are normally listed in the history books. But the historian is concerned, too, with the lives of ordinary people: the changes in their way of life, the forces that caused these changes. History is happening everywhere, all the time.

The invention of the steam engine, and its application to industrial production and to transport; the development of electric power and of electronic communications: these are some of the great forces that have revolutionised life in Ireland in the last six generations. But they were not confined to Ireland: the same forces have helped to change the pattern of life throughout the world. The man of 1780 or 1790 lived in a stable world, where change came slowly, like the melting of a glacier. The young Irishman of today lives in a world which is changing around him, very rapidly, all the time. An understanding of our own past can help us to adapt ourselves to these changes without losing our sense of identity.

I: Six Generations

From the very beginning of time, until about one hundred and forty years ago, no man was ever able to travel faster than the speed of a galloping horse. From the ancient Greeks with their war chariots to the Norman knights who followed Strongbow, and right on down to the age of Napoleon, even the great kings and conquerors of history had been limited to about fifteen miles an hour. Travellers in the early nineteenth century complained of the dangerous speed of stage coaches that covered nine miles in an hour; while people with goods to carry had to be satisfied with walking pace—perhaps four miles an hour. From Dublin to Belfast was a long day's journey; while as late as 1818 the traveller from Dublin to London, allowing for the speed of the mail coach and the vagaries of sailing ships, had to reckon at least two days for his journey.

These factors set the limits of man's world from the earliest times until about 1830. Then came the railway, and a transport revolution. Within the last 140 years our idea of distance has been revised again and again. When the railway and the steamship came into use, a man could leave Dublin late in the evening and be in London for breakfast next morning. Today in a jet plane the same journey takes less than an hour; and New York, once several weeks away across the ocean, is a matter of five or six hours from Shannon. Jet travel is shrinking the world—just as the train once did for Ireland.

During the last six generations the changes in everyday life have been extraordinarily rapid. A boy or girl still in school can remember the introduction to Ireland of television and the jet aircraft. A man of sixty might remember Alcock and Brown crash-landing near Clifden at the end of the first trans-Atlantic flight; he would certainly remember the early days of radio broadcasting. A man of eighty would have seen the first motor-cars on Irish roads, and he would remember when the bicycle was a novelty. His grandfather might well remember Ireland before the railway.

The same man—the great-great-great grandfather of the schoolboy of today—might have been born about 1790, when an Irish Parliament was sitting in the Parliament House in College Green. The building itself—now the Bank of Ireland—has changed very little, but everything around it has changed. In those days you could stand in the middle of College Green for a chat without fear of being knocked down by the traffic. Dublin then, although it was a capital, was a compact city of no more than 180,000 people. Today it has grown to a great sprawl that houses well over half a million.

The boy who was born in 1790 would have lived through the rebellion of 1798; he would have been ten years old at the time of the

James Malton's view of the Parliament House (now the Bank of Ireland) and Trinity College, Dublin, c.1793.

Act of Union, which ended the independence of the Parliament in College Green. He might have heard his parents talking of Robert Emmet; but it would have been very difficult for him to form a picture of Emmet, because the process of printing drawings was tedious and expensive, and so there were no illustrations at all in the newspapers. The newspaper editors concentrated on getting as much information as possible into their journals: there were no big headlines and everything was set out in straight columns of type. By our standards, too, the papers were very expensive: a typical one cost fourpence, which was at least equal to four shillings in our money, or half the daily wages of an unskilled workman.

Circulations also were very small. Schools were few at this period, and more than half of the Irish people could neither read nor write. A good reader often read the paper aloud for a whole group. Moreover, the language of the newspapers, English, was still a foreign language for the majority of the people. Six generations ago, two-thirds of the people spoke Irish in their daily lives. Many of these understood some English, but not more than they needed to do their business in the nearest town.

Six generations is not a long time. In many a graveyard around the country you can find headstones that go back that far: frequently you can trace back several generations of the same family. But for many other families the only monument is the ruins of abandoned houses. They remind us that, in the past, there were far more people living in Ireland than there are today. The population in the countryside has gone down steadily ever since the Famine.

Sometimes we notice a big gateway at the end of a village street. Here is the Great House, roofless and crumbling. Once it was the

"Reading the Nation": from the painting by H. McManus in the National Gallery.

residence of the landlord who owned the village and the land all around; he lived elegantly on the rents paid to him by the people in the cottages. So the ruined mansion has a story to tell—the story of a change in the social order that once ruled the countryside.

Looking around us in the country, we can see signs of the changes in industry too, in the ruins of the long-abandoned mills or factories. Much of the manufacture of goods was done in the homes of country people. Yarn was spun by the fireside; cloth was woven on a loom by a farmer. The town was a market to which the cloth was brought for sale. There were factories to finish the cloth, or to make iron goods or paper or the like; but they were in the countryside too. They had to have power to work their machinery, and this was provided by a great waterwheel. Little factories were set up anywhere there was enough water to drive a wheel. Mills were to be found at intervals down the course of any fair-sized stream.

In the 19th century steam power drove out water power. Steam power depended on coal. Coal had to be imported from Britain and, as it was expensive to transport, industry naturally centred around the east coast ports. As industry moved into the towns, it drew people with it, to take jobs in the factories. The Famine is one reason for the decline in population of the countryside; the shift of industry to the towns is another.

The towns were once small and compact. Ten generations ago, Dublin was a small city, and there was a sharp, clear boundary where the town ended and the country began. But then Dublin began to change: the houses began to reach out into the fields on the north side. We have maps of the city in 1730, Dean Swift's time, and to us it looks very small; but people were already surprised at how it was growing. Thirty years later the city was still growing, but as yet there was little sign of factories—industry was still mainly out in the countryside. Six generations ago, the city landscape began to change. Smoking factory chimneys became a common sight. The same process took place much more rapidly in Belfast. With the growth of linen manufacture and ship building it became a great industrial city. Even today it appears as the only Irish city which has fully absorbed the Industrial Revolution.

The new factories could not have caused a major change in the pattern of Irish life if there had not been a revolution in transport as well. When all goods had to be carried by horse and cart, loads were limited and the pace was slow, especially at a time when roads were generally bad. The great gentry, of course, had their private carriages; others went by stage-coach, or by Bianconi's "long cars", travelling at the furious pace of eight or nine miles an hour. As for

Two women spinning linen yarn by the fireside, a third reeling the yarn, late 18th century: from a print by Hincks in the Ulster Museum.

the poor, if they wanted to travel they went on foot. The coach was much too expensive for them; a day's wage would carry them only a few miles.

In the 18th and early 19th centuries canals were built. They could offer cheap transport for heavy cargoes such as coal, and they also ran passenger services which were slow but comfortable. But the real revolution came with the railways.

The first steam train ran in Ireland about ten years before the Famine: the line was from Dublin to Dun Laoire. Twenty years later there was a network fanning out from Dublin all over the country. Now hundreds of cartloads of goods could travel on a single train, and in a fraction of the time taken by the horse. The journey from Kilkenny to Dublin had once taken a whole day. Now, with the railway, it took three hours.

Cheap transport brought the goods from the big factories out into the countryside. They could outsell the small factories, and the

A bird's eye view of the city of Belfast, about 1860. (Ulster Museum).

small factories had to close: just as today the small shops, unable to offer goods as cheaply as the supermarket, are being forced out of business. So the whole pattern of industry shifted in favour of the big factories in the towns. Between them, steam power and the Famine altered the face of Ireland.

If we are tempted to romanticise the unspoiled life of the country people of six generations ago, it is as well to remember that, for many of them, poverty was the normal condition of life. Many lived close to the starvation line all the time. A poor family in the town might live in a tenement room or a damp cellar; in the country, their home might be a one-roomed hovel without window or chimney. Foreign travellers never failed to remark on the abject poverty they saw among the Irish, and the number of beggars they met everywhere.

We must not forget that poverty was in no way unusual at this time in Europe, or indeed in Britain. But in Ireland the horrors of the Famine, and the tremendous flow of emigration that followed it, led to a mood of bitterness and despair. Naturally, people tended to lay the entire blame for these conditions on British rule; but this is only part of the truth.

In Queen Victoria's day Britain itself was changing. Although the Industrial Revolution had come to Ireland it was unable to develop as rapidly as in England, because Ireland lacked coal and iron, the materials of the new age. In England the costs of production began to fall as the machines took over. Huge factories began to make the English cities rich and dirty. People moved from the land and crowded into the cities to work in the new factories. But in Ireland, except for Belfast, there were not enough expanding towns to offer jobs. So most of the people who moved out of the countryside went for good, to England or America.

At first, the Irish filled the lowliest jobs in the industrial society: Irishmen helped to dig out the canals of England and the London docks, and to lay the railways across America. But in cities like Boston, Philadelphia and New York, the Irish became numerous and powerful. Between 1820 and 1938 four to five million Irish migrated to America. Their descendants ran into many more millions. The money they sent home and the influence they exerted in international politics were important factors in the struggle for independence. And in 1960 the descendant of two Irish emigrant families, John Fitzgerald Kennedy, was elected President of the United States.

The locomotive Hibernia ran on the Dublin-Kingstown railway, the first line to be opened in Ireland. (Dublin Penny Journal 1834).

LOCOMOTIVE ENGINE—DUBLIN AND KINSTOWN RAILWAY.

II: Everyday Life

For the Irishman of 1790, all the ingredients of daily life were found within the bounds of his own townland. Today when we build a house the concrete blocks and the steel window-frames may come from 150 miles away, and the timber from Russia or Canada; but before the railway made transport of materials easier, houses were built of local materials. The walls were of clay or local stone. The roofing timbers were often cut locally too. The roof was made by the local craftsmen, using straw or reeds gathered in the district. Thatching is still carried out in some areas, particularly in Co. Wexford and in Adare, Co. Limerick, and the styles of thatching vary from one area to another, in accordance with the weather conditions and the materials available.

The houses our forefathers lived in varied enormously. At one extreme were the mansions of the gentry, at the other end a crude cabin made of branches resting on a bank and covered in "scraws". Many families, especially in the western half of the country, lived in one-roomed cottages, occasionally sharing the room with the cow and the pigs. Chimneys were usual in the 19th century, but there were still cabins in which the smoke from the fire had to find its way out by the door.

But it would be a mistake to think that everybody lived in these conditions. In the east and the midlands, and indeed in many parts of the west, there were many comfortable farmers who lived in well-built houses surrounded by outhouses for the livestock. Slated roofs, which had been introduced to Ireland with the Plantations, were numerous in the east; but thatched houses were common in the town as well as in the countryside. In a poor town like Kells nearly all the houses were thatched, and in large towns there were whole districts of thatched houses like the old Claddagh in Galway. Adare, in Co. Limerick, still gives us some idea of what a prosperous village would have looked like.

The heart of the household was the kitchen, and its central point was the fire. There was rarely a shortage of turf for fuel. The fire was raked out at night and built up again with fresh sods in the morning. The man of the house had the seat in the chimney corner. There was a hook over the fire, to hold the iron pot; on the dresser there were wooden plates, shiny jugs and the china mugs for the tea. There was a settle bed, used as a seat in the daytime, and a bin for the meal. The floor was sometimes paved with flagstones, and sometimes made of the bare earth. When a house was built, the neighbours would be invited in to have a dance so that the floor would be beaten down firm and flat. The windows of the house

A crude cabin in Co. Mayo, about 1860; photograph restored by George Morrison.

were small, but the half-door stood open at the top to admit the sunlight.

Churning was done in the kitchen or, in the more prosperous farms, in a dairy nearby. In the old days butter was made in a dash-churn, which was simply an upright wooden churn with a plunger inside operated by a handle extending through the lid. When the cream was poured in, the plunger was dashed up and down, and this action caused the fat to separate from the buttermilk. After about twenty minutes the butter floated to the top and was scooped out on to a saucer. The remaining milk was washed out of the butter, and then it was salted so that it would keep. The buttermilk remaining in the churn was used for baking bread.

In the evenings the room would be crowded, especially if the the farmer had a family of good-looking daughters. The local seanachaí might entertain the company with a story, or the schoolmaster might read aloud from the *Freeman's Journal*. The woman of the house would be seated on her stool, perhaps taking a pinch of snuff from time to time, and the air would be thick with the smoke of the men's pipes.

These clay pipes cost only a few pence a dozen; the favourite tobacco was twist —tobacco leaves twisted into a long roll and sold by length rather than by weight. Cigarettes were not smoked very widely until after the 1914—18 war.

Most of the household furniture and utensils were made by local craftsmen. A Donegal man said of his village then that "there were stone-masons, turners, coopers, thatchers and every sort of trades-man to be found in the town". The cooper made the churn and barrel, the turner the plates, the tinker mended the pots, and the pedlar came to the door with his basket of china-ware. The black-

A country kitchen interior: painting by Mulvaney (National Gallery).

Tossing pancakes on Shrove Tuesday: from Hall's Ireland, its scenery etc.

smith made the crane for the hearth and other household implements, as well as shoeing the horses.

For the first half of the 19th century, the men in the countryside wore a costume modelled on that of the gentry of Grattan's time: corduroy kneebreeches, knitted stockings, white linen shirt with a bright cravat, and a tailcoat in green, blue or grey. Women wore a cloak—the type of cloak which survived till recently in the neighbourhood of Kinsale—but during the century the shawl became popular. Under the cloak or shawl girls wore a skirt and bodice: the skirt, usually of red flannel, came half-way down the shin, to give freedom of movement and to let the boys admire a pretty ankle. Small children of both sexes wore petticoats, and it was a great day for a lad when he laid aside his petticoats and became a man. The womenfolk and children in poorer families often went barefoot: indeed, barefoot children were a common sight even thirty years ago.

In spite of poverty, country life was by no means dismal. The tradition of music and dancing lay deep in the souls of the people. The fiddler and piper travelled from wedding to fair, from pattern to market, and were well known and loved in their districts. Among the young men hurling was always popular—played with fifty or sixty barefoot hurlers on each team—and football also was widely played. But the games were not nationally organised until 1884, when Davin and Cusack founded the G.A.A., under the patronage of Archbishop Croke of Cashel.

At the Big House, there would have been croquet on the lawn; or cricket, with a team made up of the gentry and their tenants. There would have been musical evenings in stately rooms, and there was always a well-stocked library. Fox-hunting, shooting and fishing were always enjoyed by Irish landlords, and they had house-parties of guests to join in these rural sports; while some of them developed very fine gardens, such as those at Birr Castle.

Irishmen of all classes drank heavily. At wedding and funeral, fair and wake, the *cruiscín* was always there, and the delights of whiskey are celebrated in many a song. "Drink", went an old saying, "is a disease without shame". Beer and wine were cheap, as was legal or "Government" whiskey. But in some parts of the country—especially where cash was scarce—the most popular drink was home-distilled poteen. With the increased activity of the revenue police, and after Father Mathew's great temperance campaign in 1839, the standard of poteen began to fall, and some of what was

Donnybrook Fair, c. 1840, from Hall's Ireland, its scenery etc.

sold was dangerous firewater.

Time in the country was measured not by the calendar but by local fairs. Though the primary purpose of the fair was the buying and selling of animals, people also came to shop at the stalls. They came to the great fair of Donnybrook to dance, to matchmake, to drink in the booths, and often to fight. Faction fights were a common feature of the fairs. The fights were partly the working-out of ancient grudges between families, partly a crude and dangerous form of sport, but chiefly the result of too much drink. The good faction fighter, indeed, had the glamour of a modern sports star. His weapon was not the shillelagh that is sold to the tourist today but a stout cudgel of oak or blackthorn about three feet long. Sometimes the women joined in too, using a rock in a stocking. The challenge to fight was issued by trailing a coat along the ground and daring a rival to step on its tail: the expression "coat-trailing" is still used.

If there was one man who could stop a faction fight it was the priest. Religion was woven into the lives of the people. Sunday Mass was an important occasion, though in poor districts the Mass might be said from an "ark" with the congregation kneeling in the open air. The pilgrimage to Lough Derg drew devout pilgrims from all over the country; but generally a parish had its own annual pilgrimage, to a holy well or some place associated with a saint. The day of the pilgrimage was called the Patron or Pattern Day, and the pilgrimage was called a pattern or station. Often thousands attended, and when devotions were ended they flocked to enjoy the fun of the fair.

But the Famine cast a heavy blight over the social life of the Irish countryside. As an old Donegal woman said: "The sport and the recreations vanished. The poetry and the dancing came to an end. They lost them and forgot them, and when the good times came again those things never came back as they were before."

The city man had more sophisticated pleasures. He could go on the train to the seaside at Bray or Bettystown, or attend a concert in the Rotunda Gardens. Better still was the theatre. Most of the plays shown in the middle of the century were English comedies and melodramas, and the people in the pit loved to hiss the villain or cheer the pure heroine. Ireland's favourite dramatist was Dion Boucicault. In plays like "Arrah na Pogue" he helped to create the image of the stage-Irishman, but the mob up in the "gods" loved his plays.

Then in 1897 Edward Martin, W. B. Yeats and Lady Gregory issued the famous Coole Manifesto, proposing an Irish National

22

Theatre, which would show that "Ireland is not the home of buffoonery and easy sentiment as it has been represented, but the home of an ancient idealism". In 1899 Yeats's "Countess Cathleen" was performed at the Ancient Concert Rooms—now the Academy Cinema. (It must be added that the popular audience disliked it thoroughly.) In 1901 Douglas Hyde's Gaelic play "Casadh an tSugáin" was staged, and in 1904, with the financial assistance of the Manchester tea heiress, Alice Horniman, the Mechanics' Institute in Abbey Street—a theatre dating back to 1820—was purchased and became the Abbey Theatre.

The Ireland of the 19th century was a land of sharp contrasts: contrasts between rich and poor, between town and country. Today prosperity is spread more evenly: poverty and want have not been eliminated, but the gap between "haves" and "have-nots" is less wide.

A pattern in Connemara: engraved from a drawing by W. H. Bartlett. (National Library).

III: The Farmer

Not only in Ireland, but everywhere in the world, change comes quickly in the towns and more slowly in the countryside: very slowly indeed in the more remote country places, where farms are small and land is poor. The small farmer of to-day does many of his jobs on the farm in much the same way as his grandfather before him. The changes that you can see are more obvious on the bigger farms—especially the change from manpower and horse-power to machine-power. Farming to-day is becoming more and more like industry—making greater demands on scientific and technical skills, using giant machines that depend on modern forms of motive power like the diesel engine.

But in many ways the most important changes are the ones that are not visible: especially the changes in the ownership of the land. Most Irish farmers today own their land. But until the end of the 19th century the farmer did not own the land he farmed: he rented it from a landlord. In fact this question of land ownership was one of the basic political issues of the last century.

An old print from the Ulster Museum tells us quite a lot about Irish farming six generations ago.* In front is the farmer at his ploughing; his wife and children are calling him to a meal under a tree. In the background are the rolling parkland and the big house, with an elegant coach driving up to the door—obviously the home of a rich landlord. The plough is very crudely made of wood—only the ploughshare itself is made of iron—and it would only scratch the surface of the ground. Arthur Young, the famous traveller, wrote: "They plough generally with four horses . . . and use ploughs of so bad a construction that a man attends them with a strong stick, leaning on the beam to keep it in the ground . . . ."

In the picture too we can see another man sowing the seed by hand. Usually the ground was harrowed before sowing, to break up the soil. All of these operations—ploughing, harrowing, sowing—were slow, back-breaking work, and it took a lot of labour to produce a crop.

As time went on improved types of plough were introduced, and eventually an all-iron plough came into general use. In the 18th century the plough was generally drawn by three or four horses, but the more efficient iron plough was drawn even for heavy work by only two horses. To-day of course the tractor has largely displaced the horse, but horse-drawn ploughs can still be seen on small farms.

The plough was generally used on good ground; but the basic tool

* See frontispiece.

everywhere was the spade. It was used for all tillage work in hilly country, and even on good land it was used for trenching in potatoes. There were spade mills or factories in many districts, supplying a local market, and the type of spade they turned out varied in accordance with local needs and customs. One of these spade mills can be seen in the grounds of the Ulster Folk Museum.

In earlier times, the poor labourer walking the roads with his spade under his arm and his shoes in his hand might be met in some parts of the country. He might well be a *spailpín fánach*, a migrant labourer who travelled from the poorer districts to the richer farming areas in search of work. The first migrants made their appearance in the spring, when the ground was being broken up for tillage. Farmers

A hired labourer, c.1850: from Haevey's Sketches of the Irish Peasantry, National Library.

went to engage the migrant workers at hiring fairs; and a famous poem expresses the bitterness of the *spailpín fánach:*

Go deo deo arís
Ní raghad go Casail
Ag díol nó ag reic mo shláinte
Nó ar mhargagh na saoire im 'shuí cois falla,
Nó im 'scaoinse ar leathaobh sráide.

There was plenty of work to be done on the bigger farms during the summer season. Haymaking called for a lot of labour, and even more was needed for the harvesting. The corn was cut with a scythe; then it was bound into sheaves by hand, and the sheaves assembled into stooks. At a later stage the stooks were loaded on carts and taken to the farmyard. Women as well as men took a hand in the haymaking and harvesting, but there was still work for the casual labourer. At the end of the season he took his pay and set off again to his own place, to dig his potatoes or save his own little crop.

By the end of the 19th century the migrant workers had all but disappeared. Machines were being developed to carry out various farm operations and they greatly reduced the need for outside labour. But the poor man continued to offer his labour further afield. From Donegal and Mayo they went to Scotland, for seasonal work on the potato crops; from further south they went to the cities in search of building work, and often enough they never came back.

After the harvest, the corn had still to be threshed. This was done with a flail: the corn was spread out on a clean floor and beaten with the flail, and the beating separated the grain seeds from the chaff. Threshing like this was a slow and tedious job, and it went on at intervals right through the autumn and spring months. But threshing was one of the first farm operations to be mechanised. During the 19th century the threshing machine was introduced. Powered by a steam engine, the machine could complete the whole threshing for the season within a couple of days. The wealth of a farmer was often measured by the time it took to complete his threshing.

The threshing was quite a social occasion. Men and women worked together, and neighbours helped one another. The sheaves were pitched from the rick on to the threshing machine, where a man untied them and fed them into the machine. The machine separated the grain from the husks and fed it into sacks, which were taken away as they were filled. The straw was built into a rick, and the farmer used it as bedding for his animals.

To-day the brief, hectic excitement of the threshing has disappeared from rural life. The giant combine harvester cuts and threshes the

Threshing with a steam traction engine c. 1910. (Cooper Collection, Public Record Office of Northern Ireland, Belfast).

corn in a single operation. But the old threshing machines and the steam traction engines that worked them can still be seen in a museum at Stradbally, Co. Laois.

The steam engine was too clumsy and far too expensive to do most of the jobs about the farm, and even up to twenty years ago the farmer's main source of power continued to be the horse. Horses were needed for ploughing and also for cartage of goods. Every farmer had at least one cart. Up to the early 19th century the carts were very simple ones with solid wooden wheels; but spoked wheels, which were much lighter, became common in time, and the wheelwright, who made the spoked wheels and fitted iron tyres to them, was an important figure among rural craftsmen. On market days the towns were filled with the carts of farmers from the country-side all around. They carried the family and the neighbours to the market, and they also carried produce or animals for sale and brought home the sacks of seed or meal. A rich farmer had a trap as well, to take the family to church or to visit their neighbours, and he might well keep a good saddle-horse in his stables. A common interest in horses and an admiration for good horsemanship formed a bond among countrymen, from the gentry right down to the labourer, and at the great horse fairs all the fanciers of horseflesh matched their knowledge and skills against one another.

Mechanisation did not at first reduce the importance of the horse; if anything it increased his usefulness. Sowing and haymaking were speeded up by the use of the horse-drawn drill for sowing seed and by the mowing machine. The horse-drawn reaper and binder, introduced from America, took a lot of the labour out of harvesting. Only in the last twenty years or so has the use of the tractor significantly reduced the value of the horse in farm operations, and the number of horses in use has declined sharply. As a direct result the skills of the wheelwright, the saddler and the blacksmith are tending to die out: except where they are kept alive by the use of horses for sport and recreation.

As we know from the Penal Laws, a horse was an important item of property; and it was of course far too expensive for a poor man. For him, the donkey became in the 19th century the beast of all work. Self-reliant and hardy, the donkey lived out of doors in any weather, and foraged for himself on the hillsides. He was called into service to draw turf from the bog or to bring produce into market.

The large farmer did his tillage by horse and plough, the smallholder by hand. But for both of them, tillage was a very important part of the farm economy. A little was done everywhere, and in some areas a great deal. In general potatoes were grown for food; grain was a cash crop grown for sale. All around the country can be seen the ruins of the little mills that used to grind oats, barley or wheat for the local market. In many places too there are the remains of disused limekilns; lime was burned in these kilns and spread to improve the soil.

But in many districts farm income depended—as it does to-day— more on animals than on tillage. Ireland has always been a great cattle-producing country: right back to the days when the High Kings counted their wealth or exacted tribute in head of cattle. The great war of Irish mythology, launched by Queen Maeve of Connacht against Cuchulain and the men of Ulster, arose from a dispute over the Brown Bull of Cooley. To-day cattle are still the most important of all our exports, and some of the best beef comes from the counties which have always fed or fattened cattle— Limerick, Tipperary, Galway, Roscommon, Westmeath and Meath.

Fairs provided the opportunity for farmers, dealers and butchers to buy and sell cattle—as well as being great social occasions. They continued as an institution all around the country until the last few years, when they have been rapidly displaced by the rise of the livestock marts. These substitute a system of open auction for the old method of individual bargaining. Ballinasloe was the centre of fairs for horses, sheep and cattle, and it also had a famous wool fair; for the counties of Galway and Roscommon were at one time the greatest grazing area for sheep in the whole country.

The areas that fed cattle bought many of the animals from dairying districts. In fact one of the functions of the fair was to transfer cattle from the dairying areas, where too many calves were born in relation to the supply of grass, to other areas where not enough

A horse fair at Saintfield, Co. Down. (Welch Collection, Ulster Museum).

calves were born and farmers were eager to buy young livestock for their farms. The main dairying counties were Cork, Kerry, Waterford, Limerick and Kilkenny. Dairy cattle were also kept in the vicinity of the towns, or even in the back-streets of the towns themselves, as this was the only way in which the townspeople could hope to get fresh milk. Cows were usually milked in the open—as indeed they still are on small farms. Most of them were probably pretty miserable beasts, by the standards of to-day, and the milk yields were poor. Still, the ownership of a cow marked a boundary between really deep poverty and some modest sense of security.

The farmer with a number of cows turned the surplus milk into butter. Butter-making was not very hygienic: often the churning was done in the smoky atmosphere of the cottage kitchen. Cork was the centre of the greatest butter-producing region in the country and had a famous market from which butter was exported all over the world. But by the end of the 19th century this oversalted and often dirty butter was becoming harder to sell to the foreign consumer. The only way to save the industry was to establish creameries.

Creameries were small factories in the countryside, which extracted the butterfat from the milk and converted it into butter. Most of them were run as co-operatives, with the farmers themselves being the shareholders. Creameries emerged as focal points in the life of the dairying districts, and some have grown by now into large and efficient industries. Butter is made in clean and hygienic conditions and the farmer's wife is relieved of the labour of churning.

Tillage, sheep, cattle and dairy cows—these made up the farmer's income. The Irishman's pig, which was such a favourite joke with English humourists, was fattened on potatoes and household scraps; it was slaughtered at home and most of the flesh was smoked and salted so that it would keep, in the form of bacon and ham.

Fuel was not a great problem. For anybody who lived near the bog, there was turf for the cutting. If a town was near, there might be a cash market for turf as well. Boats brought cargoes of turf up the Shannon estuary to Limerick, and sailing boats with turf plied along the coast of Connemara. Along the west coast, seaweed was saved and burned to make kelp, which was used as a bleach for the textile industry. And in the west and north-west, especially, many of the country people made some extra cash from a strictly illegal traffic in poteen—home-distilled whiskey.

Because many of the small farmers were underemployed on their own scraps of land, they often engaged in the domestic textile industry. Wives spun the yarn and men wove the cloth. But this kind of activity, very common in the early 19th century, had almost died out by 1900, except in Donegal. On the other hand, fishing enjoyed a boom around the whole of the western coastline towards the end of the century. The small farmer was often a fisherman as well, as good a hand with the oars and nets as he was with spade and plough.

Farming conditions varied quite a lot throughout the country. The north and the eastern counties as far south as Wexford were comparatively prosperous. Wexford impressed two English visitors, Mr. and Mrs. Hall, who wrote a very famous book on Ireland: "The skilfully farmed fields, the comfortable cottages, the barns attached to every farm-yard, the well-trimmed hedgerows, the neat gardens stocked with other vegetables than potatoes . . . ."

The north, especially from Armagh to Portadown, also gave an impression of neatness and comfort: "the little farms with their orchards and comfortable buildings are as neat and clean as could be wished; they are mostly of one storey, with long thatched roofs and shining windows."

In the midlands generally, conditions were not so good. Farms were not as neat, there were more straggling cabins and more poverty. Nevertheless, there were many comfortable homes; and the range of food was much wider than in the poorest regions. Of Queen's county (now Laois) a land agent wrote: "The population of that county was never very excessive; the farms were moderate in size, and valuable as the potato was, it rarely formed (as in other districts) the sole food of the people . . . ."

Dowdall Bros. Creamery at Charleville, Co. Cork. (Lawrence Collection, National Library).

Conditions in the greater part of Munster were broadly similar to those in the midlands. It was along the west coast that conditions were really bad: in Donegal, Mayo, West Galway, Clare, South Kerry and West Cork. All these districts were supporting many times the number of people who live in them to-day, and poverty was almost universal in whole regions. Holdings of land were tiny— so small that even if they had been rent-free, the income was still too little to maintain a family. Houses were bare cabins, often without a chimney. A correspondent of *The Times* wrote in 1845: "There is not a pane of glass in the parish, nor a window of any kind in half the cottages. Some have got a hole in the wall for light, with a board to stop it up. In not one in a dozen is there a chair to sit upon, or anything whatever in the cottages beyond an iron pot and a rude bedstead with some straw on it . . . In many of them the smoke is coming out of the doorway, and they have no chimneys. The poor creatures are in the lowest degree of squalid poverty . . ."

These regional differences in prosperity are important in studying the effects of the Great Famine.

Rural living conditions

FIRST HALF OF THE NINETEENTH CENTURY

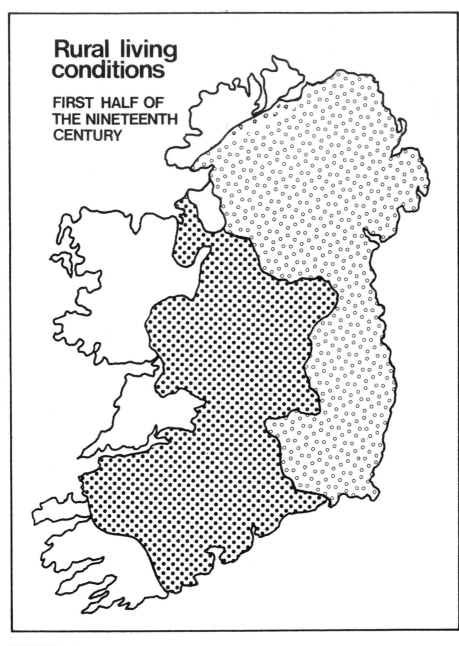

The division of Ireland into three regions as shown on the map characterises Irish agriculture in the first half of the nineteenth century. This division also foreshadows the varying incidence of the Great Famine of 1845-1848, relatively light in the east and north, serious but not general in the rural community in the mixed region, and as a rule general and disastrous in the poor region of the west and south west. In the poor region, however, west Donegal and some of the coastal districts of Kerry escaped relatively lightly during the famine years. Conditions did not remain static during the half-century. In Cavan and Monaghan, for instance, relatively prosperous at the outset of the century, the decline in the domestic linen industry was responsible for a very significant deterioration in social conditions subsequently.

 Prosperous region. Small but relatively comfortable farms. Small farmers, as a rule, predominant in the rural community.

 Mixed region. Relatively large farms, cottiers and landless labourers numerous, often outnumbering the farmers.

 Poor region. Minute subdivided holdings, and small plots of marginal land recently reclaimed from waste; extensive, often general, poverty. General absence of the social contrasts characteristic of the other two regions.

IV: Who Owned the Land?

The level of prosperity varied a great deal not only between regions, but between people of different social classes living in the same region. Hincks' print of a farmer at work, which is in the Ulster Museum, gives us an illustration of the social structure.* The man at the plough is probably the farmer himself; he is a man of some substance, since he has a team of four horses. The two men with him, one leading the horses and the other sowing, are his labourers. In the background is the Great House, which is obviously the residence of the landlord.

Here we have the different levels of society pretty clearly distinguished. The distinction would be most readily apparent in the eastern counties and the midlands. The farmer's house might be quite large and comfortable. In addition to the house itself he would have a farm-yard and outhouses. He would own one or two horses, or even more, and he might have a trap as well as a farm cart. The labourer on the other hand lived in a hovel: no more than a single room, with a bed and a fireplace. He had no outhouses, and in all probability he owned neither a horse nor a cow.

In the east, small comfortable farms were quite numerous. In the midlands, east Galway and east Munster, the farms were fewer but larger, and the labourers were poorer and more numerous. Along the west coast there were few farmers, in any real sense of the word, and few labourers working for daily wages. The majority of the inhabitants were smallholders, alike in their poverty.

At the other end of the scale is the man in the background—the landlord. Down to the end of the last century the majority of Irish farmers did not own the land they farmed; they rented it from a landlord. The conflict of interests produced by this system is one of the great underlying themes of the 19th century in Ireland.

So much political controversy centred around the landlords in the 19th century that it is difficult to form a fair judgement on them. But it seems certain that there were many who took a considerable pride and interest in their estates. Some built cottages for tenants and many built model estate villages. The town of Abbeyleix, laid out by Lord de Vesci in the mid-18th century, is a good example of the work of an "improving" landlord. The centre of the village forms a market square, with a neat market-house built by the landlord for the tenants.

The landlord of an estate like this had very great power for good or ill in his own area. In addition to being the landowner, he was usually the largest employer of labour: between servants and estate

* See frontispiece.

staff he gave work to a large number of people. And in those days, relations between landlord and tenant were often quite harmonious. Rents were probably not as high as historians have suggested, and farmers did not mind paying them as long as prices were good. What they really feared was a bad harvest; or, worse still, good harvests followed by a slump in prices. Rent only became a worry in a bad season. What the farmers really wished, as a farmer-poet wrote 200 years ago, was that "produce would be dear so that it would earn the rent". Almost a century later another farmer-poet said:

Is féadfaigh tú bheith ag ól seal,
O d'éirigh an t-arbhar daor.
("You may drink a while, since the corn has become dear").

In some areas there was local unrest over the enclosure of common land, or the creation of large farms for grazing. Sometimes this led to violence, especially the houghing and maiming of cattle—a particularly cruel form of retaliation. The feeling is vividly illustrated in this extract from an early 19th century poem.

Ag teacht an tséasúir déanfaimid sleuchta,
Marbhóchaimid céad agus dá mhíle bó,
Beidh buailí Shasan le beagán géimní
Ag teacht an tséasúir má bhíonn muid beo.
Beidh leathar fairsing ag na gréasaibh Gaolach',
'S ní iarrfaimid péire orthu níos lú ná c'róin.
Beidh bróga againne gan Dia dá méadú,
'S ní íosfaimid béile níos mó gan feoil'.

More serious, in the sense that it was more general and more lasting, was the unrest over the payment of tithes. The tithe was a kind of tax levied on farm produce for the support of the Established Church, which was, of course, the Church of Ireland. Not only Catholics, but Presbyterians, Methodists and other Dissenters were bitterly resentful of a system which put them to double expense—for they had to support their own clergy out of their own pockets, while at the same time paying tithes by law to the Church of Ireland. In a bad season the grievance became unbearable.

Though the owner of the Big House generally went to the Protestant church, he had a layman's dislike of tithes, and could sympathise with his tenants on this score. In fact, Protestant landlord and Catholic tenant were often on quite good terms. After 1790, however, the feeling began to change. In the North, unrest had been growing between Protestant and Catholic. It led to the founding of the Orange Order in 1795, and this in turn increased sectarian bitterness. Catholics in some southern counties, particularly Carlow and Wexford, feared that the Orangemen would march from the north to massacre them. On the other hand, when the 1798 rebellion broke out in Carlow and Wexford, Protestants thought that it was a religious uprising, and feared they would be murdered by the Catholics. Atrocities were in fact committed on both sides, and these added to sectarian feeling. The pictures by Cruikshank published in Maxwell's "History of the Great Rebellion" depict the Irish rebels as brutal, sub-human creatures: exaggerated as they are, they reflect the revulsion felt after the event by many of the upper classes. The confidence that had existed on both sides was seriously impaired.

The people in the Big House themselves were now divided into opposing groups. On one side there was the liberal group that favoured the movement for Catholic Emancipation; on the other, there was an "ascendancy" group bitterly opposed to Catholic claims. Daniel O'Connell's movement for Emancipation was the great political issue in the first generation of the 19th century. His campaign was supported by the liberal landlords, opposed by the "ascendancy" group. The two factions often fought one another at elections.

It is worth recalling that elections in those days were very different from the elections of today. Voting was confined to men who held property of a certain valuation. Women had no votes at all. The various election agents often handed out liberal amounts of whiskey to win votes; and, because there was no secret ballot, the landlord and the priests always knew how tenants had voted. Riot and disorder were not at all unusual on election day and feeling ran very high. In 1833 the poet Raiftearaí celebrated in these lines the defeat

Volunteers to save Captain Boycott's harvest being escorted by troops. (Irish Pictures; Illustrated London News).

of the "ascendancy" party, led by the Daly family of Dunsandle, in a Galway election:

Tá geataí Dhunsandail faoi smúit a's faoi uaigneas,
A's na Brunswickers buaidhearta mar gheall ar an sgéal,
m'impí gach maidin, go mothuimíd dúisgeadh
agus gallaibh d'a rúsgabh in gach cúinne ag na Gaeil.

When Catholic Emancipation was won in 1829 O'Connell became the hero of the Irish people; but as the landlord began to feel his privileges threatened, the gulf between him and his Catholic tenants grew wider. O'Connell's campaign for repeal of the Act of Union widened it still further, for after Emancipation the landlords became increasingly anxious to preserve the Union. For the man in the Big House times were changing. In many cases he was himself in financial difficulties. Prices had fallen sharply after the end of the Napoleonic wars in 1815. Rents were not going up steeply any more, and more of the tenants were unable to pay on time. So landlords themselves had less money to put into the management and improvement of their estates.

It is almost possible to draw a chart of the unrest on the land

Gentlemen farmers under police guard at **Mullingar Market**. (Irish Pictures; Illustrated London News).

during the 19th century and relate it to the rise and fall of farm prices. Things were fairly quiet while the war was on and prices remained high. When it ended in 1815, prices dropped and unrest increased. It died down again in the 1850s and 1860s, when farm prices rose. Then about the end of the 1870s prices fell again, as a result of foreign competition in the British market, and the hardship produced by the drop in incomes led to the outbreak of the Land War.

There were two financial burdens on the tenant farmer: tithes, which went to the Church; rents, which went to the landlord. In the past the landlord had sometimes sympathised with the tenant over payment of tithes; but, now with a political division widening between the two sides, the landlords tended to place themselves firmly on the side of the Established Church. The grievance was cleared up in 1838, when new laws reduced the amount of the tithe and tied it to the rent. But the burden of rent remained, and when prices fell it bore heavily on the tenantry.

Violence was not uncommon: most often it was directed against a farmer who dared to take over a vacant farm against the wishes of the local people. Tipperary in particular suffered severely from these agrarian disturbances, for it was a county of large farms and land-hungry men. English cartoons of the period depict the Irishman as a dangerous villain, armed to the teeth. Although such drawings may seem offensive now, they give a very good clue to the attitude of most English people—and probably many Irish landlords too—at the time.

In the years after the Famine some landlords tried to clear their estates of the poorer tenants. The reaction often was violence directed against the landlord's agent. The tenant farmer on such estates distrusted every move made by the landlord and his agent; while to the landlord, it seemed that the tenants were determined to obstruct even measures intended for their own good. Even the establishment of a model farm to instruct tenants in good farming could be a source of bitter ill-feeling, as this report shows:

> "Although a considerable portion of the land for the model farm had been vacant, yet to form a compact farm, lying well together and fit for the purposes designed, it was necessary to make several small changes and consolidations, and to remove some of the tenants whose land lay contiguous to the model farm; yet from these changes, which were absolutely necessary for the establishment of the proposed design, some ill-will appears to have been created towards Mr. Bateson, the agent."

In a case like this the tenants thought the agent callous and high-handed; while to the agent the tenants seemed obstructive and completely unappreciative of steps intended for their own welfare.

It is important not to exaggerate the extent of the unrest. Serious disturbances were localised. When the tithe question was settled in 1838 one big cause of discontent was removed. Then, in the '50s and '60s farm prices rose, so the farmers felt a sense of security and agitation died down. But around the end of the 1870s the situation changed dramatically. Britain was now importing cheap food from all over the world—especially North America. The competition forced down prices. Bad harvests—especially in 1879, the worst grain harvest in a century—made things even harder. Even the larger tenants had difficulty in meeting their rent. To make matters worse, the potatoes failed, as well as the cash crops. In the poor regions of the west, the smallholders, who normally could barely manage to stagger through from one season to the next, now faced starvation.

So bad were conditions in the west that a public relief committee was organised; relief tickets were given out, and ships of the Royal Navy transported stores to the needy islands off the West coast. A handout of food kept people from starving to death, and a repetition of the disaster of 1847 was avoided. But the demand was now growing for radical measures of reform on the land.

Michael Davitt, son of a poor family in Co. Mayo, and Charles Stewart Parnell, a Protestant landowner from Co. Wicklow, were the first to organise land agitation on a national scale. The Land League

Eviction: 'The battering ram has done its work' (Lawrence Collection, National Library).

"THE BATTERING RAM HAS DONE ITS WORK". 1772. W.L.

was establishd and quickly spread throughout the country. It advised tenants to offer landlords what they regarded as a fair rent, and, if that was not accepted, to pay nothing. The landlords replied with evictions; but evictions were met with resistance, and some-times attacks were made on the process-servers and the bailiffs. Under normal conditions landlords had been slow to evict a tenant. But the law was on their side and they were determined to resist the challenge of a tenants' organisation. Police and bailiffs were called in to evict the defaulting tenants. One landlord wrote to his agent:

> "I quite approve of you not pressing those tenants who are willing, but for illness or other causes are not able to pay more than a part of what they owe; but as to Land Leaguers and those who refuse from malice, I propose to proceed against them as quickly and as severely as the law will allow."

This in fact was economic war. The tenants were pitting their combined strength against the legal rights of the landlord, backed by the police and the law-courts. And if the landlord refused to accept the rent that was offered, the tenants had a new weapon against him. It got its name from an estate at Lough Mask, in Co. Mayo, where the agent was a certain Captain Boycott. Boycott refused to accept the rents that the tenants were prepared to offer, and proceeded to put them out of their farms. He found himself shunned and isolated by the whole community. Tradesmen who were prepared to serve him were boycotted in their turn. Soon the baker would not sell him bread, the blacksmith would not shoe his horse; he was left without a servant, indoor or outdoor. Fifty volunteers were brought in from the north to help him save his crops. A military guard escorted them to the estate while the people hooted and jeered at them. The volunteers went home, after saving

the harvest, under military and police protection, at a cost which was ten times the value of the crop; and not long afterwards the Captain himself had to leave the district—leaving his name, Boycott, to describe the most effective weapon of the Land League movement.

The Royal Irish Constabulary—first established in 1836, renamed in 1867—was active throughout rural Ireland. Landlords and their agents lived under threat of violence: they had to have police escorts before they could venture to stir from their homes. The farmer who dared to take over the land of an evicted tenant went in constant danger. To travel to market, or even to carry out the ordinary work on the land, he had to live under the muzzles of the Constabulary guns. Even so, some of them were murdered. Public meetings of the Land League were forbidden, for fear of a breach of the peace. Police patrols ranged the country, searching for arms and arresting suspects.

Meanwhile, on estates where the boycott was in operation no rents were being paid. Evicted tenants lived in temporary huts built by themselves and their supporters, while the produce of the landlord and his tenant was boycotted when it came to market.

In 1881 a new Act of Parliament gave tenants the right to apply to the courts for a rent reduction, and things became relatively quiet again for a time. But in 1886 farm prices dropped sharply; rents which had seemed reasonable a few seasons earlier were now oppressive. Discontent came sharply to the boil again. The Land League now produced a new policy, the celebrated Plan of Campaign. Advised by the League, tenants on estates where the rents were considered excessive were to lodge in the hands of trustees what was thought to be a reasonable rent; they were to offer this to the landlord not separately but in bulk; and if the money was refused, they were to pay him nothing until he came to terms. Instead they were to use their money in support of any tenant who might be evicted.

The Plan was put into effect, at one stage or other, on about 116 estates. The landlords retaliated on some estates by wholesale clearances. The tenants resisted, with the support of neighbours and Land Leaguers. Bailiffs, escorted by police and sometimes by soldiers, used battering rams to break down the doors; the tenants fought back with pitchforks and boiling water. The police were very active and sometimes the clashes were serious. The gravest of them happened at a public meeting in Mitchelstown. A police note-taker was unable to get through the crowd to a position near the platform. The police tried to clear a way for him. A struggle took place in which the police opened fire, killing three people and seriously wounding several others.

Unrest on this massive scale was confined to the bad years. But underlying it was the fact that the tenants' demand had changed. Now they were demanding not fair rent or fixity of tenure, but the ownership of the land.

The day of the big landlords with great walled-in estates was coming to an end. In the late 19th and the early 20th centuries laws were passed which enabled the tenants to buy out their holdings. In our own day nearly all Irish farmers are proprietors of the land they farm, and the landlord has all but disappeared from the Irish scene.

A social revolution in the countryside was taking place in these years. Political revolution had taken place too: the secret ballot, granted in 1872, deprived the landlord of political power in elections. But—this must be emphasised—there was no economic revolution. Tillage continued to decline; people continued to leave the countryside for the towns, or for the emigrant ship. The same forces which had changed life in Ireland during the century were operating elsewhere in the world too. The railway and the steamship were bringing wheat from the prairies of North America to dominate the British market. The same movement of population from farming into industry was happening in many countries. Ireland was one of the unlucky ones, because she had little industry at home and her people had to go abroad to seek industrial employment.

But those who remained were better off than before. The new system of land-holding and a recovery in farm prices from the 1890s onwards brought a modest but increasing prosperity to the Irish countryman at the turn of the century.

V: The Great Famine

In 1967, in the Indian province of Bihar, there was a drought which caused a famine: millions of people—perhaps as many as twelve million—died of hunger.

In many of the less developed parts of the world, famine is not just something to be read about in history books: it is a terrible visitor which may come any year. The rains fail to come at the normal season, the crops fail, and the people starve.

Still, when we in Ireland use the word famine, our minds turn immediately to the Great Famine of the years 1845 to 1848. The Great Famine was caused by the failure of the potato crop: it condemned to death a vast number of Irish people, it helped to change the pattern of living in the countryside, and it powerfully influenced the development of the United States and Canada. Not surprisingly, we think of such a great disaster as unique.

The Great Famine is unique in that it was the last famine in Ireland, and the last famine in Western Europe. But up to 1750 famine occurred from time to time both in Ireland and in other parts of Europe. The last general famine in Ireland before the catastrophe of 1845–48 occurred in the years 1740 and 1741, and in those years Ireland was only one of the countries of Western Europe where famine raged.

If you climb to the top of Killiney Hill, just outside Dublin, you can see a monument. It was built around 1741 as a relief work—to enable the starving people to earn money with which they could buy food. It reminds us that the famine of 1740–41 was just as severe in the east as in other parts of the country. The inscription on the base of the pillar reads: "Last year being hard with the poor, the walls about these hills and this monument erected by John Mapas Esq." The celebrated Folly at Castletown, between Maynooth and Celbridge, was another famine relief project.

In that period the Irish peasantry depended chiefly on grain for their diet. The famine struck because, owing to exceptional weather conditions, the grain crop failed. It was thought that if there were more stores or barns to store grain after a good harvest, there would be more food to go round in the years when the crops failed. So some of the big landlords built barns, both to provide relief work and to store grain for the future. The Conollys of Castletown, who built the Folly, also built a curious barn known as The Wonderful Barn which can be seen in the neighbourhood of Celbridge. Another barn of the same period which survives at Rathfarnham is known locally as the Bottle Tower.

The Obelisk *near Castletown 140 feet high*

The Famine of 1740—41 may have been just as serious as the Great Famine. A writer of the time spoke of "the roads spread with dead and dying bodies; mankind the colour of the docks and nettles they fed on; two or three, sometimes more on a car going to the grave, for want of bearers to carry them; and many buried in the fields and ditches where they perished". But so far, we are unable really to assess just how serious this famine was. It is scarcely mentioned in Irish history. It is only recently that historians have begun to study it, from the scanty materials available. It never left an impression on the minds of the historians, or even on the people of its own day, as the Great Famine did a hundred years later. And one wonders why.

There are several reasons. First, transport was still relatively primitive in 1740, and even as serious a disaster as widespread famine was treated as a local rather than a national event. By 1847 the great age

A famine funeral at Shepperton Lakes near Skibbereen, 1847. (Illustrated London News).

of railway building had just begun. News travelled faster: people in Dublin soon realised just how serious and how general the disaster was.

Again, there is not a single illustration of the famine of 1740–41; but by 1847 the popular illustrated magazine had arrived, and its drawings told the story of death and suffering even more vividly than words. They carried a picture of the disaster into the comfortable homes of Victorian London and they shocked the whole civilised world.

Another reason why the Great Famine remained so vivid in popular memory is that it occurred at a time when the tide of nationalism was just beginning to rise. The national hero was Daniel O'Connell. His great Repeal meetings had just taken place; his trial and triumphant acquittal had occurred in 1844; and three years later, when the Famine was at its worst, he died. A year later William Smith O'Brien organised his ill-starred rising in Tipperary. John Mitchel summed up the patriot's view of the Famine as a crime committed by the British Government against the Irish people; and Queen Victoria, who came to Ireland on a State visit in 1849, remained labelled for ever in Irish minds as the Famine Queen.

A hundred years earlier, famine had been taken for granted. Those people who commented on it—and they were remarkably few—spoke in sorrow not in anger. It was a natural disaster: an Act of God. In 1845 the Government was not only better informed about conditions, but was also better organised to provide relief. The Board of Works had been set up in 1831, the Poor Law administration in 1838. Today as we look back on the Famine, we tend to think of the relief measures as short-sighted, grudging and badly managed. In many ways this is true; but for their own time, they were an

44

Paupers clamouring for admission to the workhouse 1846.

impressive effort. At the height of the Famine, in 1847, four in ten of the population were receiving relief under the Poor Law organisation. The Great Famine is singular as the last in Western Europe. It is memorable also as the first one in which relief was organised on a national scale.

The famine of the 1840s was caused by the potato blight. Blight is a fungus disease and nowadays every farmer knows how to control it by spraying. But in 1845, when it first appeared in Ireland, it was mysterious and terrifying. Overnight, it seemed, fields of healthy potatoes turned black, as if they had been blasted by fire. When the tubers were dug they were black and rotten. Sometimes, even if the potatoes seemed quite healthy when they were dug, they went into a rotten mess in the clamps.

The disease first appeared in the late autumn of 1845. It affected certain districts only, and the early potatoes escaped completely. But in the next year the crop throughout the country was destroyed. The Famine reached its peak in 1847, in the months before the ripening of the new crop. The crop when it came was good in quality but only a fraction of the normal quantity, because the people had been without seed potatoes to plant; so famine conditions continued in many places in 1848.

To understand why the Famine was such a terrible disaster it is necessary to look at the conditions in Ireland at the time. The first important factor is the size of the population. Between 1740 and 1845 the population of this island increased very fast indeed: in a hundred years it increased almost three-fold. By 1845 it was over eight million, or twice the total population of the island to-day. Many of the people lived all the time on the verge of starvation. Their basic food was the potato.

The situation was worst in the western districts. These had been settled only thinly in the 18th century, and the population grew very rapidly indeed in the years before the Famine. Tenants scraped a bare existence out of tiny plots of land. Their homes were generally hovels grouped together in little villages. Home industry, such as weaving, had often provided a small cash income for people on poor holdings, but this had declined very much in the decade before the Famine.

Beggers were very common both in the countryside and in the towns; they followed coaches or begged at the doors of the well-to-do. To cope with the growing problem of poverty the new Poor Law was passed in 1838, and workhouses were soon being built to offer food and shelter to the destitute.

The effects of the Famine varied from one region to another, in accordance with their basic level of prosperity. In the north generally and in the east, famine as such scarcely existed, though conditions were certainly very difficult for the poor. But many died as a result of famine fever. Pestilence has always been the companion of famine, ever since the earliest times. In Ireland the fever first made its appearance in the districts where the Famine was at its worst, in the west; but it was carried into the east and north by the desperate families migrating from the west in search of food.

In the midland counties disaster was far from general, but conditions were much less satisfactory than in the east. More of the people were dependent on the potato and suffered seriously from the Famine. But it was along the seaboard of the west and south-west that the Famine left its most terrible marks. Here poverty was general even in normal times. Even in good years cash incomes were small; people lived from the produce of their own little holdings, and there were no shops or any system of buying or selling food. They depended on the potato, and when it failed there was nothing for them but starvation.

The soup kitchen organised by the Society of Friends, Cork. (Illustrated London News).

Skibbereen and Schull in west Cork; Kilrush in Co. Clare; west Galway and Mayo: these were the places where suffering was most terrible. Famine fever spread rapidly as people huddled in their homes or even in the ditches, or crowded into the towns and besieged the workhouses for admission. In Cork a report said that "the influx of paupers from all parts of this vast county was so overwhelming that, to prevent them dying in the streets, the doors of the workhouse were thrown open, and in one week 500 persons were admitted, without any provision either of space or clothing to meet so fearful an emergency. All these were suffering from famine and most of them from malignant dysentery or fever".

Even the workhouse was no refuge. Fever swept through the crowded wards: not only patients but the doctors, matrons and priests who tended them fell victims to the infection. So many died that bodies were often carted uncoffined to the grave. In towns and villages mass burials took place. In the Rocky Field at Westport rough stones mark the graves of hundreds of unidentified people; and there were many similar graveyards around the country.

In the face of this terrible disaster, what was done to help? The first to respond to the need were private individuals and religious organisations. The Quakers were especially notable for their generosity and their courage—for those who tended the sick did so at the risk of their lives, and a good many died of the fever. In London an association was formed to relieve distress in Ireland and Scotland, and Queen Victoria opened the subscription list. Irish tradition says that she gave five pounds. In fact her donation was two thousand pounds: a handsome sum for those days.

The Government accepted the responsibility of providing relief, but it was hampered by the rigid ideas of the day. Food, they said, must not be given out free because it would encourage idleness and upset the normal channels of trade. At first the Government tried to give aid in the form of employment on public relief works, but this measure soon proved ineffective. Many workers were too weak from illness or undernourishment to do a day's labour: in the worst-hit districts there were whole families in which nobody had the health and strength to work, so even when food was made available for money they had no means of buying it.

Indian corn—the "Yellow Meal" so familiar in Irish folk tradition— was imported in an attempt to fill the need for food; but it was unpopular at first because the women did not understand how to cook it, and later, when it was more familiar and the demand grew, the price went so high that it was quite out of reach of the people who were in the gravest need.

Eventually the Government abandoned the public works. Instead it gave out food at public soup kitchens, through the Poor Law administration. Other soup kitchens were set up by private organisations and by religious groups. At some of these soup kitchens, over-zealous Protestants demanded, as the price of relief, that the people should abandon their Catholic faith; and these crude attempts at proselytising have left bitter memories in some parts of the countryside. But in general the efforts of the private and religious organisations were humanitarian in the full sense.

Many thousands of Irish people had already emigrated to the United States and Canada before 1845, especially from the overcrowded districts of the West. Now, with no hope of survival in their own country, thousands more sought to escape across the Atlantic.

THE EMBARKATION, WATERLOO DOCKS LIVERPOOL

Irish emigrants leaving Liverpool Docks, 1850. (Illustrated London News).

People from the country districts tramped scores of miles to the ports, great or small, where they boarded "coffin ships" for America. Fares for the passage ranged from 50/– to £5, and passengers provided their own food. Landlords sometimes helped to provide the passage money—either because they wanted to clear the land of tenants for their own profit, or from a genuine desire to help those who left and to improve the conditions of those who were to stay behind. The average length of the voyage to an American port was 40 days, and conditions on the ships were appalling. Many of the passengers already had famine fever when they came on board: in the crowded and insanitary conditions below decks it spread like wildfire. Thousands of those who left Ireland in the hope of a new life never saw the shores of America; thousands more died soon after setting foot on land. A monument at Crosse Isle, near Quebec, bears this inscription: "In this secluded spot lie the mortal remains of 5,294 persons who, flying from pestilence and famine in Ireland in the year 1847, found in America but a grave". But many of those who survived lived on to prosper and became an important force in the life of their new country.

What of those who stayed behind? The potato crop failed again in 1848 and many more died. But gradually conditions improved, and in the east and the midlands from about 1850 onwards there was a period of almost thirty years of reasonable prosperity. Shops, once rare outside the towns, were now becoming common in rural areas too, and their goods were more varied. But along the western seaboard, where the death toll in the Great Famine had been the greatest, conditions improved very little. People still lived in wretched hovels, in dire poverty.

At the end of the 1870s the potato crop failed again. This time there was a crisis in west Galway, Mayo and Donegal, where hunger was very acute; but private and public relief measures were organised promptly and the crisis was localised—there was no danger of starvation in other parts of the country. At the terrible cost of the Great Famine, the situation had changed greatly in thirty years.

Nobody knows exactly how many people died in the Famine, but the total death toll from starvation or fever was probably about a million; another million left by emigration during those few years. For a century afterwards the population continued to fall. But even if the Great Famine had never happened, the population of Ireland would almost certainly have declined during the 19th century. In the poorer areas there were far more people living on the land than it could decently support: in some areas you can still see the shape of fields which have been untilled for a hundred years. The decline of domestic industry helped to reduce many smallholders, once comfortable enough, to a state of insecurity. These economic pressures would certainly have caused a movement of population from the country to the towns, and a considerable volume of emigration to industrialised countries that offered more opportunities of making a living. But the Famine overcame people's natural reluctance to leave their homes, and it set a pattern of emigration that persisted for generations.

It is probably true to say that the causes of the Famine were purely social and economic; but it had far-reaching political consequences. It added a new bitterness to the feelings of Irishmen towards England, and it created a great and powerful group of enemies for Britain in the United States. It is no accident that the Fenian movement of the 1860s drew its main strength from the labourer and the unskilled worker, the classes most subject to economic insecurity; nor that it established the link between the Irish at home and the Irish-Americans which was to be of such great importance in the years leading up to independence.

VI: Domestic Industry

The farmer's work has always been concerned with animals and crops. Six generations ago, the crops and animals were essentially the same as they are to-day; the operations of ploughing, sowing and harvesting are fundamentally unchanged, though the tools of the trade have been modernised. When we turn to industry, however, we find a picture which has altered totally. Indeed, we find difficulty in drawing any line at all between industry and agriculture; for the industrial worker and the farmer were generally one and the same person, and instead of the factory the centre of manufacturing was the home itself.

At the time of Grattan's Parliament, manufactured goods featured very little in the life of the ordinary man. By far the most important of them was cloth; and this was produced not in factories, but by spinners and weavers working in their own homes.

Their raw materials came directly from the land: wool from the sheep, and flax, which was rotted and "scutched" to produce linen fibres.

In the 18th century there was a large domestic market for cheap cloth, and there was also a big and growing export market in England for Irish yarn and cloth. Because the process of manufacture was slow and laborious, a huge number of people had to be employed to make all the yarn and cloth required for the home and foreign markets. Spinners and weavers were at work all over the country as the 18th century went on. Spinning in particular spread rapidly; for smallholders and labourers, the cash it brought in was a help in paying the rent, or in buying such simple luxuries as twist tobacco, clay pipes, snuff, salt and shop whiskey.

The woman of the house had her spinning wheel, and with it she spun flax or wool into yarn. The farmer or labourer himself did the tilling and sowing, and looked after the farm animals; but in the evenings, and especially in the winter, he spent his time weaving yarn into cloth.

For the country child, the sound of the spinning wheel and the clickety-clack of the loom must have been familiar from the cradle; and indeed, in poorer families the boys and girls themselves learnt to spin at an early age, and so contributed their small share to the very modest income of the family. Around the end of the 18th century there must have been a spinning wheel in almost every cabin. The types of wheel differed in different areas: in Connemara the spinner worked standing up, in the Blasket Islands she sat down. On a fine day the wheel was carried out of doors, and often the

mother and grandmother, and perhaps one or two of the big daughters, might be spinning at the same time. A man of the time records: "Me mother would come in and she in the long black cloak with the hood. She would draw the wheel to her and that was the office for me and my sisters to start carding. She would be singing to the wheel."

Spinning was a slow and tedious operation. The wool or flax had to be drawn between the index finger and the thumb into a continuous line of fibre, and the spinning wheel helped to twist the fibre so as to produce a secure and unbroken thread. Because it required no particular physical strength it was suitable work for women and even for children. The fact that spinning was done part-time by women and children helped to keep the price of yarn remarkably low, and the low price enabled it to find a ready market.

Indeed, the price of yarn was so low, and its manufacture demanded so much time, that a family could not possibly live by spinning alone. But it was welcome work because it helped to support the family income from agriculture: where no spinning was done the poverty of smallholders was often acute. The better-off families did not think it worth their while to spend their time in spinning, but sometimes the servants might spin yarn as part of their duties, under the supervision of the farmer's wife.

The north-east was the main centre of linen manufacture. But as the industry grew, the local supply of yarn was insufficient for its needs; and hence spinning spread throughout Ulster, the northern counties of Leinster, all the counties of Connacht, and right into the southern half of the country, especially Clare, Cork and parts of Kerry. The spinning of worsted yarn from wool also increased in this period: it was especially widespread in Cork, parts of Tipperary and in the Queen's County, where the town of Mountmellick grew prosperous as the centre of the trade in worsted yarn.

The districts where yarn-spinning spread rapidly were usually comparatively poor. Much of the yarn was bought by jobbers, and never came to the local markets at all. Apart from a few market towns, little record or evidence survives of the domestic spinning that was once so common in most parts of rural Ireland.

If spinning was women's work, weaving was a job for a man. The loom was a large wooden frame, which took up quite a lot of

A hand-loom weaver: the loom incorporates the "flying-shuttle", in early looms the shuttle was thrown from side to side by hand.

Waringstown, Co. Down—a hand-loom weavers' village. (Welch Collection, Ulster Museum).

space: it was often put in a separate room. In operating a hand loom the weaver had to throw the shuttle from side to side, carrying the thread of the weft between the threads of the warp. This operation required the length of a man's arm; and to carry it out again and again over a long period demanded physical strength and stamina.

Weaving was often a part-time job. But it required skill, and it also paid better than spinning; so many weavers, if they had little farming land, found it more profitable to take up full-time weaving in their own homes. The part-time weavers were at a disadvantage: they had to give much of their time to the farm, and the amount they could weave for the market was small. Moreover, they were less skilled than the full-time weaver. So gradually part-time weavers became fewer, and whole villages of full-time weavers emerged in the busier weaving districts.

At one period there were flourishing colonies of weavers in all four provinces; villages or small towns such as Monivea, Co. Galway, and Ballymahon, Co. Longford, prospered around this activity. The weaver was an independent craftsman and earned good money. Malachi Horan describes a little community of weavers who lived near him on the Killenarden Commons, not far from Tallaght. There were nine families, all related, and all from the north: "Silk and cloth weavers they were. A quiet people. They would be hawking their goods through the country here and what they couldn't sell they brought to the city. You would be seeing them in their ass carts on this road and they on their way to Thomas Street. A nice living they had and they earned it." But then came the night of the Big Wind in 1839: their looms were driven through the walls of their houses, and they left the area.

The north-east, however, was at all times the main centre of linen weaving, and it contributed to the prosperity of the towns there. Besides the weavers, other workers were employed in finishing the cloth; rich drapers and bleachers lived round about; and regular markets for linen were held in the towns. The neat and regular appearance of towns like Hillsborough, Lurgan and Lisburn still reflects their origins as centres of the linen industry.

Linen was the most important branch of the textile industry, but wool brought prosperity too. Towns like Bandon, Blarney, Dripsey and Glanworth in County Cork were all thriving centres of woollen weaving. Rathdrum in Co. Wicklow was the marketing centre for the flannel made by the farmer-weavers of the Wicklow hills. Woollen cloth was finished in little "tuck mills", scattered throughout the country, especially where the supply of water was ample for washing the cloth and driving the finishing machinery.

After weaving, linen cloth was sold to a draper, who then handed it over to a bleacher for finishing. First the woven cloth had to be "beetled"—that is, pounded by flat beaters which were worked by a water-wheel. This was in effect a factory process, carried out by quite elaborate machinery in a large building. Then the cloth had to be bleached, to take out its natural dirty-brown colour and turn it to the dazzling white that was demanded by the market. This was done by repeatedly washing the cloth and laying it out for days at a time on a bleach green, to be bleached by daylight. A watchman was employed to guard the green against thieves at night. Both the finishing factory and the bleaching green itself were quite substantial pieces of property, and the bleacher who owned them would be a wealthy merchant.

As the industry grew, a whole structure of markets developed to distribute the cloth to the customers. The woven cloth was sold to the drapers at local markets throughout the north-east. After bleaching, much of it was then sent for sale at the great Linen Hall in Dublin—then the greatest cloth market in Ireland and one of the foremost in Europe. The Linen Hall itself has long since gone, but

A bleaching green; from Hall's Ireland, its scenery, character, etc.

the streets round about still bear witness to its old associations—
Coleraine Street, Lisburn Street, Lurgan Street. In 1783 Belfast
built its own Linen Hall and less of the trade then came south to
Dublin. But still it was the capital provided by the Dublin merchants
which helped to make the expansion of the industry possible.

In the 19th century the domestic system was replaced by factory
industry; power spinning replaced the spinning wheel, power looms
took over the work of the hand loom. But in poor and remote areas,
where labour was cheap and farming too impoverished to be a full-
time occupation, the old methods still survived. The spinning wheel
was still in use in some areas—notably Donegal—in the late
19th century. The tradition of weaving on the hand loom has
survived to the present day, and Donegal tweeds woven by the old

process are in demand throughout the world. Some other hand crafts actually grew in importance during the 19th century, especially in the north-west. Many a Donegal mother helped to support her family by knitting stockings or by the fine hand-embroidery for which the women of the area were famous.

Spinning and weaving, and to a lesser extent knitting and sewing, were by far the most widespread forms of domestic industry. But at one time even the blacksmith did his work at home, in a little forge adjoining his house. A hearth with a fire of coke or coals, a bellows worked by hand to fan the fire, and an anvil on which to hammer the heated iron into shape—these were his main tools. The smith made and fitted horseshoes, but he also made gates, nails, hinges, and all kinds of farm implements, With the wide distribution of factory-made articles, he was reduced to shoeing horses as his sole activity; and now, when so few horses are employed in farming, most of the forges have closed their doors for the last time.

Basically, the domestic industries were built on the strength of a man's arm and the skill of a woman's fingers. They became obsolete when new and more powerful sources of energy became available: when men harnessed to industry the power of moving water and the power of steam.

Dublin Linen Hall; from a print by Hincks, Royal Dublin Society.

VII: Water Power

Modern industrial society was born in the 18th and 19th centuries. Its growth depended on the development of new and more sophisticated forms of energy for application to industry. Water power gave way to steam power; the machinery of industry grew larger and more complex, and industry in the home gave way to the mill, the works and the factory.

The idea of harnessing water to work for man goes back to very early times. Centuries ago the Egyptians used the running waters of the Nile to turn a primitive water wheel. The Syrians, the Greeks, the Chinese all harnessed water power to help them to grind their corn, raise water from the rivers or work bellows for forges where iron was worked. The water wheel they employed was a simple one which lay on its side and projected into the river just enough to catch the current which made it turn. Wheels like these became common throughout Northern Europe: they were called Danish wheels, in the belief that they had been introduced to these islands by the Norse invaders. They were still used fairly widely until the 19th century.

It was the Romans who developed the type of water wheel we know best today—that is, the wheel which stands upright in the stream. The Romans used their water mills almost entirely for grinding corn, and at the beginning of the 19th century in Ireland also you could find water mills for grinding corn in almost every district.

The primitive method of grinding corn was the quern, a very simple machine consisting of two round flat stones. The bottom stone was fixed, the upper one was turned by hand. Grain was poured through a hole in the upper stone and was crushed into meal or flour by the friction between the two stones.

The quern could produce only a small amount of flour because the crushing surface was small, and the top stone could only revolve as fast as the power of a maid's hands could drive it. But when the water wheel was harnessed, by means of cogs and gears, it was able to drive much larger stones and to turn them much more rapidly. At Old Ross, near Wexford, you can see one of the handful of old water-mills still in use. There has been a mill on this site ever since the Normans came to Ireland 700 years ago, but the present structure dates back only 120 years, to 1848. When the miller raises the sluice gates the water of the mill stream pours over the top of the wheel; it fills the buckets and the wheel begins to turn—slowly at first, then gathering speed. Inside, the grain is poured from a sack through a hopper on to the mill stones. It takes about five minutes for the mill to grind one bag of meal; with a quern it would be difficult to fill a bag in a day.

The grain mill at Old Ross, Co. Wexford.

When this mill was built there were almost two thousand mills in the country, scattered along the courses of the rivers. In many towns where no relic of the mill itself is left there is still a Mill Street. But in many districts the ruins of the old mills are still to be seen—sometimes at the end of the main street of a village. Today they are often roofless, covered with ivy, their windows broken and their big wheels gone. There were many mills along the banks of the Nore—remains of them can be seen at Bennetsbridge and Thomastown; and a mill still working at Lucan is a reminder that a number of them lay along the Liffey too.

Early mills were simple buildings one or two storeys high, but often they were rebuilt as time went on, and at the time of the Famine even the small country mills were as a rule at least three storeys high. The grain was hauled up to the top floor in sacks by means of a winch worked off the water wheel. From there it was fed downwards again by gravity into the hopper, as it was required for milling.

Some of the Irish mills were large enough to impress even the English visitor. The earliest of these structures was at Slane, on the Boyne, where one of the buildings is still in use as part of a modern cotton factory. The great weir and the massive masonry walls were erected two hundred years ago, to direct the powerful flow of the Boyne into a canal or headrace leading to the water wheel. Similar mills were built along the banks of canals or navigable rivers or in the heart of the prosperous grain districts.

Tillage declined sharply in the last quarter of the 19th century and the little mills began to close. Grain was imported now, and it was ground into flour or animal feeding stuffs in the great mills that were built at the larger ports, using steam engines as their motive power.

The wind is another natural source of energy which has been used since very ancient times to drive millstones. For centuries windmills were a common sight in Ireland, on level ground where the wind blew steadily. Indeed a number of windmills were working up to about fifty years ago. The towers or stumps of old windmills are still

The gears turned by the water wheel at the Old Ross mill.

to be seen in areas such as South Wexford, where the land was level, and the strong and regular breeze compensated for the fact that there were few streams swift enough to turn a water wheel. There were even a few windmills in the suburbs of Dublin, and some of them were still at work at the time of the '98 rebellion. Two stumps of old windmills are still to be seen in central Dublin—one inside the present boundaries of Guinness's brewery and the other close to the South Wall. At Ballycopeland. Co. Down, there is an old windmill which is preserved by the National Trust.

Water was, of course, much more reliable than wind as a source of power, and therefore the water mill was much more important than the windmill to the development of Irish industry. Water wheels were not confined to grinding corn; indeed in the 18th century water power was increasingly used to drive other types of machinery. In the textile industry, in particular, large and elaborate machines were being introduced, and these had to be housed in large buildings. Belfast was in an ideal position to use water power, because of the swift streams flowing down the hills which flank it on the west; and by the beginning of the 19th century many cotton spinning mills had been established in this area.

Mills to finish woollen cloth were set up at this time also. There were little industrial complexes at villages like Glanmire, near Cork; Blarney whose ten mills included a woollen mill, a corn mill and an ironworks; and Beechmount, which had a paper factory, ironworks

The Monard spade mill, Co. Cork, in the 1930's. (Photograph by courtesy of A. R. Day).

and foundry. All of these depended on plentiful water power.

Ironworks on a large scale were to be found in or near several of the large towns on the east coast. But more modest ironworks, making simple agricultural tools like spades, were to be found in many parts of the country. One of these simple spade mills, still in working order, can be seen in the Ulster Folk Museum. The water wheel is used here, by means of a simple device, to make the great hammer rise and fall. The smith shapes the spade by moving the red-hot metal plate around under the blows of the hammer. The Monard Spade Mill, at Blarney, operated continuously for 200 years, giving work to six generations of Blarney families; the sound of its great hammer ceased ringing through the narrow valley only ten years ago. Unlike many other small ironworks, it was slow in succumbing to the big factories that came with the age of steam.

Even before the steam age, then, at the beginning of the 19th century, quite large and complicated machinery was being used in Irish industry—especially in the textile industry, and it was driven by water power. Unlike the spinning wheel and the hand loom, this machinery could not be used in an ordinary home; large factories had to be built to house it. And these had to be located beside streams or rivers where there was power to drive the water wheels. So the worker could no longer do his job at home. Now he had to go out to work at the mill, and houses had to be provided for him near his work.

Some industries needed more workers than others. In corn milling, iron working, paper making and cloth finishing a handful of skilled men were enough to carry out all the operations. But in spinning and weaving mills, where the processes were more complicated, more workers were needed. Even after factory spinning was introduced, workers were needed to look after the machines and to prepare the fibres for spinning.

Some of the early factory owners built model villages to attract workers. The ruins of one of them can be seen at Stratford-on-Slaney; it was built at the time of Grattan's Parliament to house workers for the textile factory whose ruins can still be traced in a neighbouring field. Another model village, built in Co. Kildare in 1780, was called Prosperous. The name itself is an index of the confidence that people felt that new ventures like this would succeed in the countryside. In 1780 people did not foresee the difficulties that lay not very far ahead of them, in the age of steam.

Sullivan's paper manufactory, ironworks and foundry at Beechmount, Co. Cork. (Cork Public Museum).

VIII: Steam Power

Not far from Heuston Station in Dublin, there is the stump of a tower; once a windmill, but now stripped of its sails. It is a reminder of a period when wind and water were the main sources of energy. But wind and water were not reliable enough to sustain an ever-increasing demand for power for industry. This factor and others hastened the search for a new, more efficient, more constant source of power.

The steam engine came to satisfy this need. Men had experimented with steam as a source of energy even in the distant past: Hero of Alexandria describes a kind of steam engine in the early Christian era. But the Greeks felt no pressing need for a new source of power, and in any case their technology was not advanced enough to build large working models. So from Hero to the 17th century there was little progress to report.

During the 17th century began the real search for a method of harnessing the power of steam. At this time there was an urgent demand for coal and metals. To satisfy it, miners began to tunnel more deeply into the ground. One of the hazards of mining is flooding. As the mines became deeper, the existing pumps were not powerful enough to get rid of the water; so engineers had to find a new source of power to work the pumps.

In 1698 an English military engineer, Thomas Savery, patented an ingenious steam pump; it was used for exhibition and for pumping water for country mansions, but it had great practical disadvantages. Denis Papin, a French engineer, developed a more useful design, using steam to operate a piston inside a cylinder. Papin's design had its first practical application when an Englishman, Thomas Newcomen, adapted it to a pumping engine in 1712.

Newcomen's engine had a boiler to heat the water, a cylinder into which the steam was channelled in successive blasts, and a piston. The piston rod was attached to one end of a great pivoted beam, and the pumping rods to the other end. The up and down movement of the piston moved the beam up and down, and this movement was transferred to the pumping rods at the other end. By 1725 this "fire engine for raising water", or "atmospheric engine", was in common use, and it held the stage for nearly three-quarters of a century. In 1769 there were 57 Newcomen engines in coal mines in the Newcastle area alone. The first engine in Ireland was erected on the Kilkenny coalfield in 1741, but there appear to have been no steam engines elsewhere in the country until the 1780s.

The Newcomen engine was useful only for functions involving an

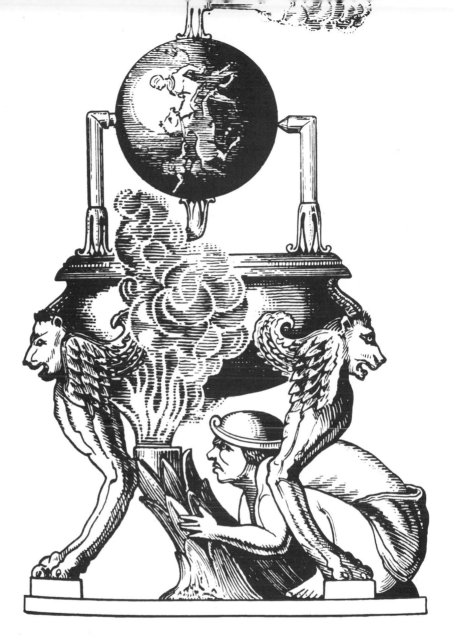

Hero's reaction steam turbine or 'aelopile'; (Dean's Engines for Power and Speed).

up-and-down motion—that is, for pumping. If a steam engine was to be used to operate other kinds of machinery, then some way had to be devised of linking it to a rotating shaft. The breakthrough came in 1781 when the Scottish engineer James Watt adapted the Newcomen engine to rotary motion.

Watt kept the great beam, but he attached a crank to the rod at what had been the pumping end of the beam. This in turn was attached to a shaft, in such a way that the up-and-down motion of the piston was transferred as a rotary motion to the shaft. A

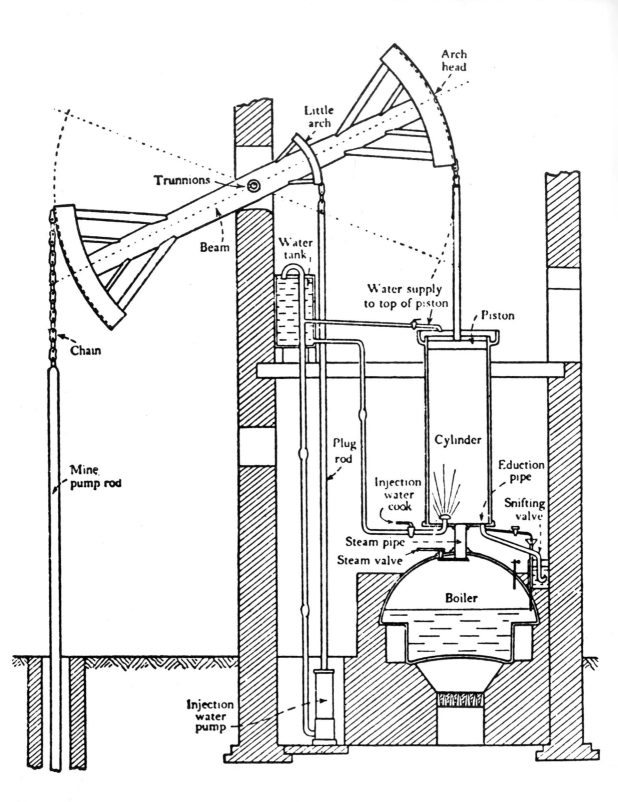

heavy flywheel attached to the shaft helped to ensure an even and continuous motion. The steam engine was now developed to a point at which it could replace the water wheel in driving factory machinery. Further developments took place during the 19th century, as the great beam disappeared and the piston and driving shaft were directly connected by the crank. So the steam engine was not the invention of one particular man in one particular year. It was evolved gradually to meet the needs of a society eager for new sources of power.

Steam power was produced by boilers, which were normally fired by coal. England had plenty of coal, and its industry developed rapidly. Ireland had some coal—mines were worked at Arigna, in Co. Leitrim and at Castlecomer, Co. Kilkenny—but the supply was

Watt's double-acting rotative engine. (Dean's Engines for Power and Speed).

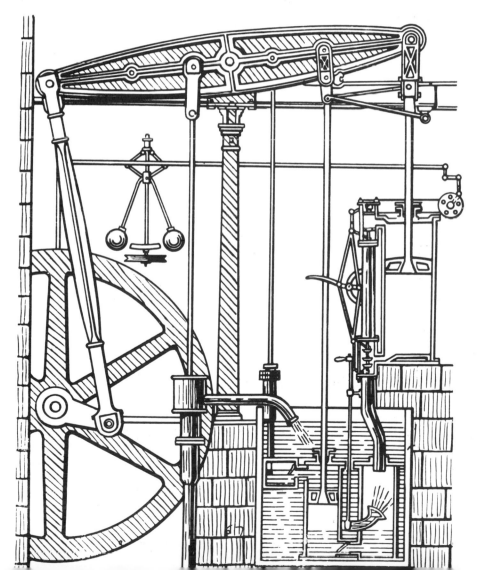

Newcomen's Atmospheric Engine, 1712. (A History of Technology, vol. iv., edited by Charles Singer, E. J. Holmyard, A. R. Hall, and Trevor I. Williams).

small and the cost of production was high. So the coal for Irish steam engines had to be imported from England; and, as it was costly to transport, Irish industry in the 19th century came to be centred around the ports nearest to Britain, especially Dublin and Belfast.

The tall factory chimney, belching out its black smoke, is the symbol of the 19th century. The mills and factories of the steam age, lying at the foot of these massive chimneys, were gaunt and uncompromising, with little windows lining their many storeys and grimy brick walls. Small houses for the workers clustered around them.

New machines and greater power vastly increased the output of industry. The revolution was especially rapid in the textile industry Machines like Arkwright's Water Frame, Crompton's Mule, and, much later, the power loom were introduced; they changed the textile industry in Ulster from a home industry to one based on the factory. Instead of being scattered through the province, textile manufacture was now concentrated on Belfast, where imported fuel was cheaper, transport to and from the factory cost less, and there was no difficulty in attracting labour.

The same factors combined to draw other industries towards the east coast towns. Up to 120 years ago Belfast had no special reputation for shipbuilding; ships were built around the coast at any suitable site. But with the development of the iron ship and the use of steam, the shipbuilding industry in Belfast expanded very rapidly to become the biggest employer of male labour in the city.

Changes in the pattern of industry were not of course confined to the north. In Dublin six or seven generations ago there were 55 breweries; nine of them were in James's Street alone, and there were thirteen on or near the present site of Guinness's. Most of them were small—Guinness's output in 1830 was 40,000 barrels a year. But through the century the expansion of Guinness coincided with the closing down of smaller breweries in the rest of the country. Because Guinness could sell more it could sell more cheaply. By the end of the century Guinness was selling 1,750,000 barrels a year; the industrial giant had arrived.

The steam engine alone does not account for the industrial revolution. Improvements in communications, roads, railways, canals, ships, buildings all played their part. Brewing, distilling, linen and shipbuilding were the Irish industries which acquired an international reputation in the age of steam. At one time the firms engaged in these manufactures had been small and scattered through the country; but in the 19th century they became associated with particular areas. Irish linen came to mean linen from Ulster, or even Belfast; shipbuilding came to mean Harland and Wolff. Jacobs in

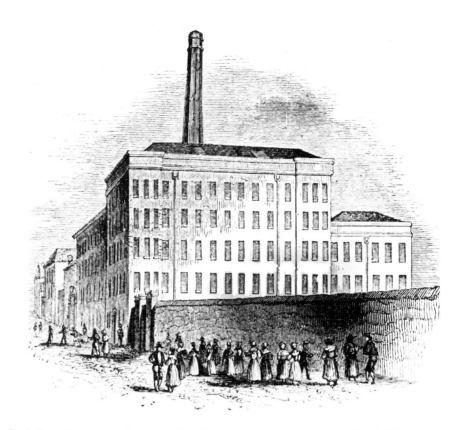

Dublin dominated the biscuit market, and instead of Irish beer people (outside the Cork region) spoke of Guinness. The success of some firms and areas meant the decline of others; the rules of competition were severe in 19th century commerce.

The decline of domestic industry meant that many country people could no longer make ends meet; so they left the land and moved into the town, to work for wages in the new factories. In Ireland, industry did not develop quickly enough to absorb all the people who were forced to leave the land, and many thousands of them emigrated to the industrial towns of Britain and America. Only Belfast, with its thriving industries, had a pattern of growth that compared with the industial towns of Lancashire or the English Midlands.

Streets of little red-brick houses were thrown up hastily, to house the troops of workers who were needed now at the shipyards and the mills. For most of them, life must have been grim enough. The factory, the church and the public-house were the fixed points of their existence. Hours of work were long—a man commonly worked twelve hours a day, six days a week. Women and sometimes

Guinness's Brewery at St. James's Gate, Dublin, early 19th century.

children worked in the factories too. Because of the pressure of competition, employers had to produce the goods as cheaply as possible, and this meant that they paid as little in wages as the workers would accept.

It was in these circumstances that trade unions were formed, to defend the workers and to secure better wages and conditions by collective bargaining. The masses in the cities threw up a new kind of leader: men of working-class origin who derived their power from the strength of organised workers. In Ireland the great names are James Connolly and Big Jim Larkin. A vivid picture of the Dublin of Larkin's day can be found in James Plunkett's novel, "Strumpet City".

The steam engine is as important in history as the discovery of the wheel. Steam power changed the face of Europe, turning its people from countrymen into townsmen. It sharply increased the contrast between the industrial nations of the West and the poorer and still largely rural nations of Africa and Asia. It built up enormous wealth in the principal industrial nations and gave them a position of dominance in the affairs of the world.

Steam power was neither good nor bad in itself. Like a horse, it could pull either a gun-carriage or a plough. It did both.

70

IX: The Towns before the Steam Age

Athlone in Irish is *Áth Luain*, or Luan's Ford: the name of the town gives a key to its original reason for existence. At this point there was a ford across the river Shannon: travellers moving from Leinster into Connacht and back went this way: probably an inn was set up, a few trading booths, a forge to shoe the horses—and you had the nucleus of a town.

Town have not sprung up by chance in haphazard locations. Very often, as in this case, there are clear physical reasons for their establishment in a particular place. By studying the location of the town we can get a good idea of the motives of its founders; and sometimes the name itself gives us the clue. Athlone, Athenry, Drogheda, Foxford, Banbridge and Newbridge are all towns set up at river crossings, by a ford or bridge, where travellers would naturally tend to meet. Similarly where a mountain range forms a barrier, the path across it would naturally go by a pass or a break in the mountains, and this is the point where a town would be likely to grow: Graiguenamanagh affords an instance.

Sometimes an aerial photograph will show up physical factors which are not so obvious at ground level. The town of Kilmallock, for instance, is grouped around the cross-roads, where the northern road from Limerick, the southern roads from Cork and Fermoy, the eastern road from Kilkenny and the western road from Newcastle West all meet. It was the site of an early monastery, which probably, like many others, offered a resting-place for travellers. Then perhaps an inn was opened, then a few shops, and gradually a town appeared.

The sea, of course, is an older highway than any road. The main port towns have grown up where the sea lanes from England and Europe met the roads from the interior: where there was a sheltered harbour for shipping, and where a great river valley provided access to a rich hinterland. Cork, Waterford and Limerick are all typical examples of the port towns. In many cases the towns were built by foreign invaders. To them the port town was a trading post on the shore of a foreign country, and it had to be in a position which could be easily defended against the hostile natives. Dublin was founded by the Norsemen on the first piece of high ground they met on their way up the Liffey—the hill where Christ Church Cathedral still stands—and just above the river crossing. King John's Castle at Limerick, founded by the Normans, guarded the port and the crossing of the Shannon.

The role of the town as a defensive position has ceased to be of any importance, but the physical factors that determined its location are

Kilmallock, Co. Limerick:
aerial photograph by
Independent Newspapers.

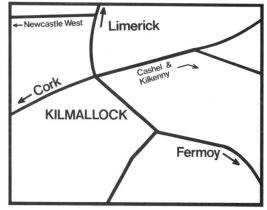

still of some importance in the part it plays in the life of a community. "All roads", said the old proverb, "lead to Rome". First of all, towns provide the commercial contact between the rural community and the outside world; secondly they play an ecclesiastical role, in catering for the spiritual needs of people; and thirdly they become administrative centres.

In a market town like Mullingar, the centre of a big agricultural area, trade with the surrounding countryside is the main business of life, and the main streets are full of shops, banks, and insurance offices. Vans or lorries from Dublin, Belfast or Cork are constantly seen—a pointer to the active commercial role of the town, but also an indication of a change in the pattern of trading. In an age of slower

72

transport goods came down the rivers and canals and were stock-piled in large warehouses for distribution by wholesalers. Today most of the warehouses are in ruins—the railway and the motor lorry have made them redundant.

The town was not only a place where the farmer came to buy: he also came to sell. Most towns had regular fairs, and nowadays, when the cattle mart has more or less wiped out the fair, the fair-green survives as a reminder of the great social and commercial importance of these periodic gatherings. The growth of the livestock industry gave a great stimulus to the growth of many towns. Ballinasloe grew around its fairs for sheep, cattle, horses and wool in the 18th century, while 25 miles away the once proud town of Athenry declined.

Some towns grew up around monasteries and churches. In most of Christendom the Church became organised in bishoprics, and the bishop's see and the cathedral were located in the most important town of the diocese. But in Ireland towns developed very late, by European standards. In early Christian times there were very few of them, and the division of the country into dioceses, for ecclesiastical administration, came centuries before its division into counties. Later the sees were connected with towns. If you study the names of Irish dioceses, and then find where the bishop actually lives, you will learn an interesting lesson about the growth and decay of Irish towns. The Bishop of Ardagh and Clonmacnoise now lives in Longford, the Bishop of Killala in Ballina, the Bishop of Ossory in Kilkenny, the Bishop of Elphin in Sligo. In many cases the original see has declined into a mere village: how many people could find Achonry?

As the importance of these towns declined, the bishops moved to others from which the administration of their dioceses would become easier. This brings us to the third role of the town—administration.

Usually a town is the administrative centre for its area. A small town has a garda barracks, schools, a post office, possibly a welfare office and an E.S.B. office. A county town has a much greater concentration of offices, including the County Hall, seat of the County Council. There will be a court house, indicating the role of the town as the centre for administration of justice in the county, with an attendant flock of solicitors' offices. There will be a main post office, a garda barracks and until recent times a county jail.

In older times the town was often a stronghold designed to enable the conquerors to hold their territory: the great castle of the De Lacys at Trim is an example. Later, during the days of British rule, a number of towns had garrisons which could be deployed, if neces-

St. Laurence's Gate,
Drogheda.

sary, to put down unrest in the surrounding country. There are big
barracks at Fermoy and Tipperary, now in ruins, and one at Mullingar
which is still in use.

The castle and the barracks remind us that, in the past, life in Ireland
was often turbulent. The towns were the centres of an alien administration, incurring the hostility of many a Gaelic chief. Small
wonder then that the merchant and the bishop, the lord and the
bailiff, the tax gatherer and the citizen, chose to live together within
the protection of a great wall strengthened by towers and gates.
This was true not only in the Middle Ages but also in the 17th
century, when the building of fortifications reached a scale un-
equalled in the past.

Limerick, Cork and Galway are three towns that had extensive walls
at this period. The Spanish Arch in Galway, one of several arches
supporting a gun emplacement, is the only relic of the fortifications
that survives. In many other towns small sections of the old walls

can still be found. A section of the old wall of Dublin, restored at a later date, can be seen beside St. Audeon's Church. Derry of course still has a ring of walls built by the London Company after the Ulster Plantation to defend their new town. At Athenry one can see a gate belonging to the old walls, and another very fine gate survives at Drogheda.

Even where the walls have vanished their memory often remains in the names of streets. At Galway we have William's Gate and Abbey-gate Street. At New Ross the name Three Bullet Gate still commemorates fortifications that have long since disappeared.

Within the walls the towns were small and compact, their towers and spires rising abruptly from the green countryside. Houses, shops and workshops huddled together in a network of narrow streets. Some Irish towns still retain a good deal of their medieval character: in Kilkenny or Athenry, for instance, you can still wander through a maze of lanes and narrow streets. Usually they radiated from a central open space which was the market place and fair-green. The Bull Ring of Wexford, the market squares at Kells and Tuam— each with its market cross—and the junction of Main Guard Street and High Street in Galway: each of these was the focus of social and commercial life in its own town.

There was no distinction between commercial and residential districts in the towns. Merchants and craftsmen lived over their

High St., Belfast, about 1786. (Ulster Museum).

shops. In the High Street at Belfast, even six generations ago, every facet of Belfast life was still represented. Shops were relatively few, and those that existed tended to sell luxury goods. The average housewife made her ordinary purchases from the street traders. Off the main streets ran narrow alleyways crowded with artisan and labouring families—a household to every room. Alleys of this kind can still be found off the High Street in Belfast; another example is Buttermilk Lane, in the heart of Galway.

Street names can reveal a lot of information about the history of a street and the activities which once centred on it. Weavers Square in Dublin and Wind Mill Lane in New Ross tell their own story. Lombard Street in Galway is the place where the Lombards, or Italian merchants, once lived.

Within the towns, most of the important buildings were of stone. When Galway was rebuilt after the great fire at the end of the 15th century, many magnificent stone houses were erected, like the celebrated Lynch's Castle. Kilmallock had many fine houses; so had Kilkenny, where one of the best examples, Rothe House, has recently been restored. But the bulk of the medieval houses were of wood, and they were often wiped out by fire, a constant hazard in the medieval town. They have now disappeared altogether. In the late 17th and 18th centuries the surviving wooden houses were replaced by stone buildings, or more often by houses made of a new cheap, all-purpose building material—brick. Most of Dublin's priceless Georgian heritage, the elegant streets and squares now threatened with destruction, was built of brick.

In the old towns the central streets were narrow, because there was very little wheeled traffic within the walls. The approach roads to the town were often wide, however, because heavy traffic passed along them to the town; and markets were held along these roads. In Dublin, the line of High Street widened beyond the walls into Thomas Street and James's Street. Here lived the merchants who supplied the city with its most vital commodity—corn. Here arose the breweries and distilleries which put the grain to another use.

In New Ross we can find the same pattern. The narrow streets of the old town broadened outside the walls into the wide sweep of Irishtown. Bohermore in Galway—the *bóthar mór*—was the wide approach road along which carts and livestock came in to supply the town.

The typical town in the 17th century, then, had narrow streets inside the walls and broad approach roads outside. But in the 18th century every elegant family wanted to have its own carriage, and wheeled traffic increased. The older streets, too, had combined residence with commerce—even a substantial merchant lived in the house where he did his business. But now people wanted to avoid the noisy central areas. Dublin expanded on either side of the Liffey into wide squares and streets which were purely residential in character.

Waterford too had its elegant residential suburb, Newtown. Similar developments happened in other towns. The great wave of building continued into the early 19th century. Our towns are full of houses built 150 to 200 years ago. They can be recognised, as a rule, by the design of the upper storeys; the ground floor has often been changed, perhaps by the addition of a shop front to what began life as a private residence. So the centre of gravity of the towns was changed by

Buttermilk Lane, Galway (Bord Fáilte Éireann).

WEST VIEW OF MERRION-SQUARE.
from the Serpentine Walk, Including Leinster House Clare st.&c.

wheeled traffic and the fashion of living away from one's work.

Another profound change was taking place in the port towns. In Dublin, ships used to come right up to Essex Bridge to moor beside the Custom House, which was just below the Castle. The river Liffey was subject to a centuries-old process of silting up; its main channel was too shallow for the larger ships. Sometimes they had to lie lower down the river and unload their cargoes into lighters. In the 1780s, the new Custom House—a splendid piece of classical architecture—was built by Thomas Gandon. So in less than a century the port of Dublin had moved downstream from its medieval site. To increase the scouring action of the river and so prevent the silting of the channel, North and South Walls were built at the river mouth, reaching out into the shallows. In 1791 Carlisle Bridge (widened later and renamed O'Connell Bridge) was built and large ships could no longer move upstream. In recent times, with a great increase in the size of ships, the main port of Dublin has moved further towards the sea.

Other ports were less fortunate. Youghal, once one of the most important ports in Ireland, lost most of its trade to Cork, in part because the channel of the river Blackwater was silting up, in part simply because Cork's businessmen were becoming richer and more successful.

Today the pattern of change in the towns is much more rapid than ever before. This is a good time to take careful stock of a town, before the changes have wiped out far more of the traces of history.

X: Development of the Towns

At Christchurch Place, Dublin, archaeologists of the National Museum have uncovered evidence of the first Dubliners. They have discovered traces of houses and streets, household utensils and ornaments used a thousand years ago on this spot by the people of the Danish city of Dublin. The houses that have been demolished to clear the site were built about six generations ago, in the reign of George III. They in their turn had replaced wooden houses built in the time of Elizabeth. A city constantly obscures its own past as it grows and changes. Within a few more years the remains of Viking Dublin will be covered again by the foundations of the new City Hall.

Archaeologists looking into the distant past work by excavation. The historian uses different materials: mainly written records of various kinds, registers of merchants and householders, electoral rolls, parish registers. Naturally these are scanty if we look far back, but they are fairly plentiful as we come nearer to our own day. It is certainly possible to form a very comprehensive picture of life in the towns and cities during the last 150 years.

In 1841 only 12% of the people of Ireland lived in towns. By 1911 the proportion of town-dwellers had risen to one third. Today, about half of the Irish people live in towns of over 1,500 population. The movement from the countryside to the towns is worldwide, and it can be expected to continue.

Not all Irish town grew in population. Some, like Kinsale and Kilrush, have declined very sharply in the past hundred years. Others like Dundalk and Galway have grown, while some, such as Roscommon and Naas, have in the long run changed very little. Moreover individual towns have experienced changes of fortune within the last century. Galway declined in the second half of the 19th century but has doubled its population in the 20th. The most spectacular growth has been that of Belfast: from being only the fifth town in Ireland six generations ago, it grew to be as large as greater Dublin within four generations.

Changes have not been confined to growth or decay; there have been great changes within the towns themselves. After the Famine the number of shops greatly increased. By the late 19th century white bread, tea and sugar—all shop-bought goods—had become staple items of diet. In the towns of an earlier age, as we have said, ordinary people bought mainly from street traders: the shops were few and they sold luxuries to the rich. But the railways made it possible to move mass-produced goods quickly and cheaply to the towns, and they developed quickly as shopping centres.

The Custom House and Corn Exchange, Dublin, about 1820: engraving by H. Brocas (Dublin Civic Museum).

After the railways came, the smaller provincial towns tended to lose their importance as centres of wholesale distribution. Instead Dublin and Belfast became the wholesale centres for most of the country, and tended to monopolise most of the import-export trade. To handle this increased traffic the ports of Dublin and Belfast expanded very rapidly. Both of them had grown up around artificial channels, carved through the sandbanks of the Liffey and Lagan respectively. The work of reclaiming the land behind the channels has gone on continuously for 150 years, and the reclaimed land stretches out to sea as a great complex of basins, docks, power stations and tank-farms.

Steam ships made their appearance in cross-channel traffic as early as 1815, but they needed to carry so much coal that they were at first uneconomic for bulk cargoes; so the steamers were used for mail and passenger traffic only, and most of the vessels using Irish ports, up to the closing decades of the last century, were sailing ships.

Up to 1818 the mail and passenger service from Holyhead docked at Ringsend. At that date the new harbour at Howth was completed

80

and became the terminal of the service; a new road was built from Howth to Dublin. But the harbour in Howth soon proved unsatisfactory owing to silting, and in 1834 the terminal of the Holyhead route was moved to Kingstown (as Dun Laoire was called after 1821). A few years earlier the reconstruction of the London-Holyhead road had been completed under the guidance of the great engineer Thomas Telford. In turn this road itself was superseded by the extension of the railway line from London to Holyhead, and after 1860 the sea crossing was speeded up by the introduction of the famous fast paddle-steamers. The first turbine boat, the Princess Maud, was put into service early in this century.

The large towns became the centres of industry as well as commerce. Five or six generations ago many small towns were thriving industrial centres. For instance, Kilbeggan five generations ago had a brewery, a large distillery, two grain mills and a tobacco manufactory. A generation or two further back weavers were busy in the immediate vicinity of the town. The distillery lasted until twenty years ago, but all the others have long since vanished. Edenderry too was the centre of a weaving district and had a brewery and a tannery. Street names again provide a clue to the past: many towns have a Distillery Road or a Brewery Lane. New Ross has a Sugar-House Lane as a memorial to a sugar refinery which flourished six generations ago.

In the battle for markets, smaller industrial centres were wiped out by

The opening of the Victoria channel in Belfast Harbour, 1849 (Illustrated London News).

larger ones. In Dublin itself many industries succumbed to English competition. But because the railways gave them a national market many Dublin industries survived: indeed, Dublin beer, whiskey and biscuits won an international reputation.

But it was Belfast which became the favourite child of the Industrial Age. The first textile mills grew up on the streams to the west of the town; and in the steam age, the inertia of tradition kept them on the same sites. Textiles were the basis of Belfast's rapid growth: ship-building came later. The Harland and Wolff yard was opened at Queen's Island in the 1850s, on land reclaimed from the sandbanks when the Victoria channel was excavated. Workman and Clark's yard was opened later on the Antrim bank of the Lagan. At first marine engines were imported, but from 1880 onwards the skill which had been acquired in building textile machinery was applied with equal success to marine engines.

These are some of the ways in which the town developed as a place to work in. As a place to live in it was changing also. In the Georgian period the rich and powerful were already moving away from the narrow streets of the old walled city. Districts like the Liberties—the quarter just outside the walls of old Dublin, where the weavers and other craftsmen lived—degenerated into slums. Later on, in the 19th century, the same fate overtook fashionable areas of the north side—Henrietta Street, Dominick Street and Mountjoy Square—as the wealthy residents moved further out. Houses intended for a single family—with, of course, its small army of servants—were converted into tenements with a family packed into each room. The *Irish Times* wrote in 1914: "We did not know that nearly 28,000 of our fellow citizens live in dwellings which even the Corporation admits to be unfit for human habitation. Nearly a third of our population so live that from dawn to dark it is without clean-liness, privacy or self-respect."

Obviously there had been nothing like enough new building to cope with the increase in the city's population. One reason for the poor standard of housing was that, even in Dublin, industrial employment was limited. Well-paid jobs were scarce outside a handful of large firms, and few of these had a big labour force. Most men earned their living by casual labour at the docks, in carting or on building sites. Handling methods at the docks were primitive, and both Dublin and Belfast required a lot of casual and unskilled labour. The Belfast textile mills provided regular, if badly paid, work for women, so a wife or daughter could supplement the family income. In Dublin there was some work for women, making clothes, or in the biscuit or cigarette factories, but there were not nearly enough jobs to go around; and in places like Cork or Galway

opportunities **were fewer** still. **In the 1890s casual labourers** earned only about 12/− a week, and many families lived at starvation level all the time. At that time only skilled workers were organised into protective unions; the great majority—the unskilled and semi-skilled—were not unionised at all.

As districts near the city centre became slums, the more prosperous citizens moved outwards. In Belfast the well-off moved to higher ground along the line of the Malone Road. Though the population of Cork scarcely changed in the 19th century, the city grew by the development of more agreeable residential areas along both sides of the valley of the Lee. Dublin had reached the ring of the canals by 1840, and it continued to spread. Neighbouring villages like Drumcondra, Glasnevin, Finglas and Raheny to the north of the Royal Canal, and Rathmines, Rathgar, Terenure and Sandymount

to the south of the Grand Canal, have long since been absorbed into the built-up area. Often you can find dates built into the houses in these suburbs, giving you a kind of water-mark of expansion.

New methods of transport were partly the cause and partly the result of the expansion of the towns. Hackney carriages and sedan chairs had answered the needs of the smaller cities of the 18th century, in which a man was never more than walking distance from his own door. The expanding city needed a cheap system of public transport. It came with the introduction of the horse-drawn omnibus in the 19th century. Horse-drawn trams appeared in the 1870s in Dublin, Belfast and other cities. Steam trams ran on two Dublin suburban routes: one linked Terenure with Tallaght and Blessington, the other ran to Lucan. In 1896 the electric tram was introduced, and soon places like Blackrock and Dartry were connected by a regular service with Sackville Street. From 1898 there were electric trams in Cork, linking outlying places like Douglas—then a simple country village—with the terminus at the Father Mathew statue in Patrick Street. Motor buses came later and eventually replaced the trams.

But it was the suburban railway which made it possible for many of the middle classes to realise a Victorian dream—to work in the city and live by the sea. In the age of railways Kingstown, Bray and Greystones, to the south of Dublin, grew enormously. The age of the dormitory suburb and the commuter had arrived.

The motor car has led to a vast new extension of the towns. Now their tendrils reach out in all directions along the approach roads and spread more and more widely across the countryside. New suburban communities, some of them as big as cities themselves, are growing up all round the fringes of the old city. Slum clearance, motor transport and electric power have altered the centre of gravity of Dublin again within the last two or three generations. Factories, freed from dependence on dockside coal, are moving away from the centre to establish themselves among the workers in the great new centres of population at Cabra, Kimmage, Crumlin, Ballyfermot, Finglas and Ballymun.

The centre of the city has altered too, as concrete and glass take over from brick and stone. The problem for the future is to adapt the city to the needs of modern living without obliterating all that it enshrines of our history and our tradition.

The expansion of the city: an aerial view of northern Dublin towards the Ballymun housing estate.

Anglesea Market, in Cole's Lane, at the junction of Henry St. and Great Britain St.

"DARKEST DUBLIN"

These pictures are part of a collection of photographs taken in 1913, to illustrate evidence given before the committee on housing conditions in the slums of Dublin. (The Royal Society of Antiquaries of Ireland).

A rear view of Gloucester Place shows how Georgian houses in the city centre had degenerated into slums as the railway and the trams enabled the prosperous middle-classes to move outwards into the suburbs.

Plunkett's Cotts, off Townsend St.

Forbes' Cottages, in Forbes' Lane, overshadowed by industrial buildings.

A tenement in the Coombe, let furnished at a rent of 4s. 1d. a week.

An unfurnished tenement in Francis St.—rent 1s. 6d. a week.

An unfurnished room in
Newmarket, let at a rent
of 1s. 9d. a week.

A group of Dublin boys photographed on their own doorstep.

Two barefoot boys: the
picture appears to have
been taken in the
photographer's studio.

XI: Social Conditions

Throughout at least the first four of our six generations, a great part of the Irish people lived in the shadow of poverty. Probably at least a third of them were very poor indeed; many more lived in conditions which were considered adequate at the time, but would denote serious poverty today. And poverty itself led to many other evils. Poor people were unable to get proper food, and because of undernourishment they were more liable to illness. They could afford only very low rents, and the result was bad and overcrowded living conditions.

Statistics tell us little, but we can judge poverty in more concrete terms. Today it is taken for granted that everyone wears shoes. But in the Ireland of six generations ago, barefooted men and women were quite a common sight. By the end of the 19th century barefooted adults were rarely seen, although children without shoes, even in winter, were still to be seen everywhere.

After the Famine living conditions improved a great deal in the countryside, but there was less improvement for the poor of the towns. Their clothing and even food were probably better than they had been in previous generations, but housing was still wretchedly bad. Off the principal streets there were narrow lanes of tiny houses, with a gutter or drain flowing down the middle of each lane. In the central areas the substantial houses of three and four storeys, built for the well-to-do, were gradually taken over by the poor—a family to each room.

In the Dublin of Dean Swift's time, the well-off merchants were still living in the narrow streets of the old city. But later in the 18th century, the prosperous citizens moved out into the new squares and wide streets that had been built around the fringes of the old town—places like Mountjoy Square or Merrion Square. As the 19th century went on, and as transport improved, the rich migrated further out again—to new townships growing up in areas that had been open fields a century before. And, each time the rich moved outwards, the areas they left were taken over by the poor, and gradually many of them became slums. By the late 19th century, Dublin had at its heart a great slumland, ringed by large comfortable residential districts. Within the municipal area about a third of the people lived in slum conditions; and three out of four slum families lived in a single room. Some rehousing was undertaken in the late 19th century by philanthropists, building societies and public bodies, but the main work of slum clearance and rehousing was not tackled until after 1922.

Bad housing was in itself an evil, but it was made much more danger-

Bull Alley, Dublin, c. 1900 (Lawrence Collection, National Library).

ous by a defective water-supply and inadequate drainage. In fact, even tolerably good houses were health hazards where there were no drains. In Belfast most of the housing, apart from that in the lanes and entries near the centre of the city, was built after 1830. These early houses, with a kitchen and living-room downstairs and three small bedrooms upstairs, were quite comfortable by the standards of their period, but they represented just as great a health hazard as the more overcrowded homes. The privy was in an outside yard, which was walled in, so that refuse could be removed only by taking it through the house. There was no public refuse service; privies and backyards were rarely cleaned, and every yard was a breeding ground for disease.

The water-closet was introduced to middle-class homes during the 19th century, but instead of solving the problem this only made it more acute. The only sewers existing in the towns had been designed to carry off rain and flood-water, so the water-closets had to be connected to private cesspools. From these the liquid matter percolated through the soil or the walls of other buildings, extending

Women and **girls** working in a spinning mill about 1900. (Photograph by courtesy of George Morrison).

the danger of infection. In time sewers were built to take away private waste; but as these discharged into the rivers, the pollution of the Liffey was appalling.

Between 1892 and 1906, a gigantic system of main or intercepting sewers was laid: one runs along each bank of the Liffey, taking the discharge from the secondary sewers. The northern one passes by tunnel under the Liffey and joins the southern one, which continues to the pumping station on Pigeon House road. From there the waste is pumped out to sea. As the city expanded other drainage works became necessary: among them are the North Dublin scheme, which discharges into the sea by a tunnel under Howth Head, and the Dodder Drainage Scheme.

Improvements in health and drainage are closely linked with an

1913: Strikers' families with parcels of food, following the arrival of a relief ship (Workers' Union of Ireland).

improved water-supply. Norse Dublin used the pure waters of the river Poddle, which flows into the Liffey by a conduit under Dublin Castle. In medieval times, the flow of the Poddle was supplemented by a link with the Dodder, and water was fed to the Old City Basin near St. James's Street. Important citizens could have water piped to their houses for sixpence a year. In the 16th century an open water-course flowed in a wooden channel through Thomas Street. Most households, however, drew their water from wells, or from fountains fed from the public supply; and these were often polluted by the effluent from drains and cesspools. As the city grew the supply of water became more inadequate. The flow of water at the public fountains was often available only for a few hours a day, and men selling water from carts were a common sight. In Dublin in 1860 many families still had to carry water over half a mile to their homes. About that time, however, major schemes were launched to improve the supply. The river Vartry in Co. Wicklow was dammed to create a huge reservoir; the water from the reservoir was purified in filter beds and carried to the city in two great pipelines. Pure and abundant water, taken for granted in any Irish town today, is in fact a blessing which only the last three generations have enjoyed.

Overcrowded and undernourished, with bad sanitation and inadequate water, the poor of the towns were inevitably the victims of epidemic diseases. Two of the great killers were typhoid fever, spread by contaminated water supplies, and typhus, spread by the lice which multiplied on unwashed bodies. Tuberculosis, or consumption, was especially dreaded among the poor: underfed people, particularly the young, were most vulnerable to the infection, and it spread rapidly in the overcrowded tenements. The Medical Officer of Health in Belfast wrote in 1909 that "consumption was most prevalent among the poor, owing largely to the unfavourable conditions under which necessity compels them to live—such as dark, ill-ventilated houses and insanitary habits, together with insufficient food and clothing". James Connolly wrote in 1905 that "the slaughter of Dublin's poor gives the Irish metropolis its unenviable and hateful notoriety among civilised nations".

Better sanitation, pure water and improved personal hygiene have played a big part in reducing the toll of infectious diseases; but Ireland has benefited too, of course, by the great advances in medical science which have been made during the last century. Vaccination has almost wiped out such diseases as smallpox, cholera, and typhoid; diphtheria, once a terrible killer of children, is comparatively rare; and tuberculosis, once the scourge of the poor, has lost much of its terror as a result of better institutional care and the use of BCG vaccine. These forms of protection have been made available throughout the whole community by means of the public health services.

Six generations ago, no form of public health service existed. Hospitals were few, and even doctors were practically unknown in rural areas. The provision of services for the sick was tied up at first with the relief of poverty. In 1838 some three or four Poor Law districts were established in each county, and each district had its workhouse, which provided shelter and food to the destitute. In its own way this was an advance; but the conditions in the workhouses were bitterly resented. When a family entered the workhouse its members were separated: there were separate quarters for men and women and for boys and girls. Each group had a dormitory, consisting of a central passage with a raised platform at either side; on these platforms were placed the straw mattresses of the inmates. The workhouse also provided medical attention, and each one had its hospital wing. The workhouses had a bad reputation, partly because the stigma of poverty attached to them, partly because of memories of the horrors of the Famine. But with all their faults they represented the first effort to deal effectively at national level with illness and poverty.

In the present century hospital services have developed enormously. Cottage hospitals deal with minor illnesses; county hospitals provide more specialised care, including major surgery; and regional hospitals offer highly specialised treatment. But sometimes a link still exists with the past, in that the new hospital is built on the site of the old workhouse.

In the early part of this century, the poor of the towns were trapped

Big Jim Larkin addressing
a strike meeting.

in a vicious circle made up of unemployment, poverty and slum
living. Conditions were not so bad in Belfast, where there was
plenty of well paid employment in manufacturing industry, and
where the flourishing textile industry offered jobs for women and
girls, to supplement the family income. But Dublin depended less
on manufacturing than on commerce and administration. Casual
employment on the docks or in labouring was the mainstay of most
families in the slum districts. Because wages were low and uncertain, families could pay only a very low rent; and on such rents
the private landlord could make a profit only by providing the very

ana being chaired by strikers.

lowest standard of housing and crowding a family into every room.

Skilled workers were better paid and more securely employed, and they could afford better living conditions for their families. Often too they were members of trade unions. But trade unions for casual or unskilled workers were something new, and the employers were determined not to recognise them. It was this clash which caused the bitterness of the trade disputes in the early years of this century. In Dublin, where James Larkin was enrolling the casual and un-skilled men in his Irish Transport and General Workers Union, the longest strike of all took place. The single issue involved was the refusal of the employers to recognise the union. Led by William Martin Murphy, the employers agreed among themselves not to admit the men to work unless they signed an undertaking to leave (or not to join) the union. The lock-out lasted from August, 1913, to January, 1914, through a winter of very severe hardship. To help feed the families of the strikers, trade unionists in other countries subscribed to send food-ships to Dublin. The dispute was both bitter and violent. Non-union workers were attacked by strikers; in turn the police baton-charged indiscriminately. To protect the workers, James Connolly formed the Citizen Army. Two years later, in 1916, he led it out to join Pearse and the Irish Volunteers in the Easter Rising.

XII: Transport

In the National Gallery of Ireland there is ⁊
Tottenham, M.P. for New Ross in the old ⊦'
College Green. He has just ridden sixty Irish ⋔.
cast the deciding vote against handing over the
surplus to England in 1731. He rushed into the Chamᵁᵉ
still in his riding clothes, and so he earned the nickname "Totteⁿ.
in his boots".

For the people of his own time, what was memorable about this
incident was that Tottenham, by his dramatic arrival, managed to
snatch a parliamentary victory for his own side. They thought
nothing at all about the fact that he had travelled on horseback all
the way from New Ross to Dublin—and at night, at that. The post-
boys of the time, who carried the mail from Dublin to the post towns
in the provinces, made similar journeys on horseback regularly. Of
course, nobody made a journey like this—about ninety of our
standard miles—on one horse all the way. They changed horses
every thirty miles or so at posts or stations: hence the name post-
boy, and the modern term post. Generally the posting station was
an inn, where the traveller could get a meal or a bed; while in the
big stable yard his horse was fed and groomed, and a fresh horse
from the stables was got ready to carry him on the next stage of
his journey.

Six generations ago, Irish roads were pretty rough, by our standards,
but they compared quite favourably with the roads in England at
the same period. Arthur Young, who travelled the country widely,
declared: "For a country so far behind us to have got suddenly
so much the start of us, in the article of roads, is a spectacle that
cannot fail to strike the British traveller exceedingly".

Most of the traffic on the country roads consisted of local farm carts,
but it was not uncommon to see carts carrying goods over long
distances. Carts brought flour into Dublin from all parts of the
country; carts with linen came down from the north to the great
Linen Hall in Dublin. Sometimes eight or nine horses and carts
were strung together on the road, under the care of a single carter.

Many individual travellers went on horseback until the end of the
18th century. But already the roads were getting better and the
gentry were beginning to travel in their private carriages. The big
development in public transport, however, was the introduction of
stage coaches, which ran on regular routes at regular times, and on
which anybody could take a place by paying his fare.

The stage coaches were great heavy vehicles drawn by four horses,

Charles Tottenham "in his boots": portrait attributed to James Latham. (National Gallery).

and carrying passengers inside and out. They ran only on the main roads, between principal towns: and the fares, though cheap by comparison with the hire of a hackney carriage, were far too high for ordinary people. It took an Italian, Charles Bianconi, to develop a coaching service that was both widespread geographically and inexpensive enough for the ordinary traveller.

Bianconi's story is a romance in itself. He came to Ireland as a penniless boy from Italy and travelled over the country on foot as a

A Bianconi car at top speed, 1834: aquatint by M. A. Hayes (National Library).

pedlar selling religious pictures. His own travels must have given him an idea of the kind of transport service the country needed. He opened up in 1815—the year of the Battle of Waterloo—with a service between Clonmel and Cahir. It was a modest enough affair— a two-wheeled car drawn by a single horse and carrying six passengers. But as his service expanded, the busier routes were served by four-wheeled vehicles drawn by three or four horses.

The Bians, as they were called, carried up to twenty passengers, and because his service was reliable he often secured a contract to carry the mails as well. The cars were open to the weather, and when it rained the passengers were provided with oilcloths which covered their knees and came up to their chests. Five generations ago Bianconi's cars were an institution throughout the south, west and midlands of Ireland. They had two advantages. They offered transport on routes where there had been no service previously; and they were inexpensive enough to be within the reach of farmers and others who, though not poor, were not particularly well off. When the railways came Bianconi withdrew his cars from the main routes and ran them as feeders to the railway. In areas where the railways were not built until late in the century they were still running in the 1880s.

Of course, with only two- or four-wheeled carts the movement of goods in bulk was tedious. A single horse could haul a few hundred-weight in a cart. But it could haul a great deal more if the weight was being supported by water; that is, if the load was in a barge on a canal. So the construction of canals was advanced as a means of improving the carriage of heavy goods across the country. As a matter of fact the very first canal in these islands was the Newry canal, opened in 1742 so that coal from the mines on the shores of Lough Neagh could be carried to Newry for shipment to Dublin. Not much coal was supplied and the venture was not very successful.

The most important canals were the Grand and the Royal, both linking Dublin with the Shannon. The Grand Canal went by Sallins and Tullamore to strike the Shannon at Shannon Harbour. The Royal, a rival enterprise, took a more northerly route by Mullingar and reached the river just west of Longford. From both of these points, of course, the river provided a waterway right down to Limerick. The Grand Canal had a spur which went off at Robertstown and joined the river Barrow, leading to Waterford. The Royal Canal was abandoned years ago and is choked with weeds, but the Grand is still open for pleasure boats; and the first few miles of its course form one of the most attractive features of central Dublin.

The canals moved bulk goods cheaply: turf, bricks and flour into Dublin; coal and beer from Dublin to the country. Warehouses to store goods for the canal traffic were built at intermediate towns, such as Rathangan; and some towns such as Tullamore had quite large canal basins, suggesting a considerable volume of traffic.

There were passenger barges as well: and from the passenger's point of view this form of transport had a lot to commend it. The barges moved smoothly through the water—unlike the lurching, heaving stage coach. There were two comfortable cabins, one for each class, to shelter passengers from the weather; and meals were served on board. A traveller of 1805 describes with satisfaction the "excellent dinner on board, consisting of a leg of boiled mutton, a turkey, ham, vegetables, porter and a pint of wine each at four shillings and tenpence a head".

The so-called fly-boats, introduced in 1834, were hauled by three or four horses and sped through the midlands at ten miles an hour— a mile or two faster than the swiftest coaches. A passenger could get from Dublin to the Shannon in a day, starting at four o'clock in the morning and arriving at ten at night.

Hotels for travellers were built at Dublin, Sallins, Robertstown, Tullamore and Shannon Harbour: the Dublin hotel, now a nursing home, still stands beside Portobello Bridge, by a canal harbour which was filled in only within the last few years.

A passenger barge on the Grand Canal at Harcourt Lock, Dublin, late 18th century. (National Library).

The construction of the canals was quite an impressive feat of engineering, but by the standards of the day it cost a colossal sum of money. The Royal Canal had cost £315,000 by the time it reached Newcastle, 22 miles from Dublin. But the financiers were convinced that they would be handsomely repaid by the stimulus the canals would give to the trade of the country. In the 1830s the passenger boats were carrying 500 passengers a day. The stage coaches too were at their peak. But that decade saw the arrival of a new invention which was to make them both obsolete: the railway.

The first steam locomotive ran from Westland Row to Kingstown— now Dun Laoire—in 1834. Ten or fifteen years later, railway building was really getting under way: from Dublin the lines fanned out to Cork, Galway and Belfast. Tunnels were driven through the hillsides and bridges thrown across the rivers. To complete the line between Belfast and Dublin a huge viaduct across the Boyne at Drogheda was opened in 1855.

The trains were still not very fast by modern standards: forty miles an hour was regarded as a great speed on the Irish railways in the 1880s. But they were more comfortable, cheaper and a great deal faster than any other conveyance. From Dublin to Cork was a 17-hour journey by the fastest coach. The railway cut it to eight, then six, then four hours. Dublin was no more than six or seven hours by rail from any town of importance in Ireland.

Quite suddenly, travel became a simple matter. People began to make journeys not only for business but for pleasure. New hotels were built at places like Killarney and Sligo to cater for the tourists; and branch lines were pushed out optimistically to places as remote as Achill and the Dingle Peninsula.

All the railways focussed on Dublin; and through Dublin the traveller could cross the Irish Sea and join the railway again from

Holyhead to London. Even before the railway, steam ships had been introduced, and these made the crossing a great deal easier. In the days of sail, the packet often had to wait days for a favourable wind, and the crossing was disagreeable, uncertain and even dangerous. But the steamers were independent of the wind: they ran to a timetable. Now a passenger could eat his dinner in Galway, be whisked up to Dublin by the train; step straight on to a ship and eat his supper on board; take the train again at Holyhead, and be in London in time for breakfast.

The railways killed the passenger traffic on the canals, though some goods traffic continued until a few years ago; and of course, they killed the mail coach. But the horse continued to play a vital role in transport for long years after the railways were firmly established. Bianconi's horse-cars ran as a supplement to the railways right up to the 1880s, and for another generation after that local transport depended on horse-carts and pony-traps. In the city you could travel in a horse-bus, or if you wanted private transport you could hire an outside car or a cab. And horse-drawn drays were used to distribute heavy goods—especially beer—until quite recently.

In the end, what made both horse-power and steam-power obsolete was the internal combustion engine. The first cars reached Ireland in the early years of this century: a famous motor-race was held here as early as 1904. The big development in motor transport came after the first World War, when mass production methods brought the cost of cars within the reach of ordinary citizens.

The growth of motor traffic hit the railways hard. The last lines to be built—in remote areas like west Kerry and Connemara—were the first to close. In the past twenty years branch lines in much more prosperous areas have been closed too: all over the country you can see the beds where the tracks were laid, and the abandoned stations. Apart from a basic network of railway lines, all our transport now goes by road. Main roads have been widened and improved, to cope with this heavy traffic, and on the whole it moves fast and smoothly; but in the towns, and especially in Dublin, a street network that was built to cope with horse-carts is being choked by an unmanageable mass of motor cars.

The internal combustion engine enabled man to realise an age-old ambition—to fly. The Wright Brothers made the first flight in a heavier-than-air machine at Kitty Hawk in 1903. The first World War caused a tremendous spurt in the development of the aeroplane; and the year after it ended a converted bomber made the first flight across the Atlantic. A monument near Clifden marks the spot where the aviators, Alcock and Brown, made their crash-landing in 1919—just over fifty years ago. Today there are trans-Atlantic crossings from Shannon every day of the year; and the time from Shannon to New York is about five hours. Charles Tottenham's ride from New Ross to Dublin might have taken him nine hours. In the same time the Irishman of today could be in Chicago.

Ward's Hill, Dublin, about 1900 (Lawrence Collection, National Library).

XIII: Communications and Energy

One of the most far-reaching developments of the present century, both in economic and in social terms, has been the advent of electricity. A hundred years ago, energy had to be transported in its primary form—as coal, turf or wood; and all these fuels were bulky and expensive to transport by road or canal. The cost of transport put the more remote locations at a great disadvantage when they found themselves in competition with industries based close to the quayside where the coal was unloaded. But energy in the form of electric current, generated from coal, oil, turf or water power, can be transported by wires as effortlessly as a telephone message.

The main form of energy for industry 200 years ago was water power. When industry changed over to steam power, coal was used to fire the boilers, and most of it was imported. So factories tended to grow up in the seaports, where coal was cheap because it came direct by sea. Industries in the inland towns were at a disadvantage: they had to pay more for their coal because of the cost of carriage. Right through the 19th century, a skyline of smoking factory chimneys was an index of industrial prosperity. Coal fires in private houses added their quota to the grime that hung over the city.

Ireland's own fuel was turf. The countryman depended on it to boil his pot and keep the house warm; the big turf fire, burning day and night, was very much the heart of the home in rural Ireland. If a man owned a bit of bog he cut and saved the turf himself, so his fires cost him little or nothing in cash terms. It was another story if he lived at a distance from the bogs: turf carted in for sale, or even brought by boat, was scarce and expensive.

Lighting in the home was provided by tallow candles, made of purified beef or mutton fat. But a big change came in the latter half of the 19th century. The paraffin lamp was introduced, and this brought a completely new standard of lighting to country people; while homes in the city were being illuminated by gas, distributed to the houses by means of underground pipes. Gas for street lighting was usual in the bigger towns by 1850, and it must have made a great difference in lightening the gloom of the Victorian streets. The problem was the system of distribution: because of the cost of laying pipes you could only have gas where there were a lot of consumers close together—that is, in the town. Today, gas is still used a lot in towns for cooking and heating, though electricity has replaced it as a source of light.

Electricity was introduced to Ireland in the last two decades of the 19th century. The first producers were industrial firms, using electricity to light the works and selling the surplus to a handful of

An early advertisement for the E.S.B., June 1928.

Stamp issued to mark the opening of the Shannon Scheme 1930.

private consumers. The trams in the big cities—formerly drawn by horses—were converted to electricity from 1896 onwards. By 1900 Dublin Corporation already had a small generating station in Fleet Street. But it was only after the Pigeon House power station was opened for the Corporation in July, 1903, that enough power became available for the needs of the city.

At first nobody thought in terms of a national power supply: development was on a local level only, and as a result it was slow and haphazard. Some Dublin suburbs still had no electricity at all as late as 1925. In all there were something like 300 small and uncoordinated generating stations scattered through the country, and many towns and villages had no supply at all. It was not until the 1920s that serious attention was given to the concept of a national electricity network. Such a network obviously demanded the building of a massive power station. The solution—long advocated by a few far-sighted people—was to plant a great hydro-electric power station on the river Shannon. Ireland's industrial development had been held back for more than a century because industry depended for energy on imported coal. The Shannon Scheme was the grand plan which was to give Ireland a new and efficient source of power.

A site was chosen at Ardnacrusha, below Lough Derg. Below Killaloe part of the flow of water from the river was diverted through a canal and fed into great pipes, where it was directed sharply downwards to gain speed. The force of the rushing water turned the turbines to drive the dynamoes which generated electricity.

The Shannon Scheme was the greatest work of civil engineering ever undertaken in Ireland. The head-race alone, which brought

Bartley Harrington, a letter-carrier in Co. Leitrim, about 1860: Photograph by courtesy of Shane Flynn, and Coimisiún Béaloideasa Éireann.

the water to the turbines, was a canal deep enough to float a sea-going ship. The Electricity Supply Board was set up in 1927 by the State, to organise a supply of electricity on a national scale, and over the next two or three years its poles and cables extended out over the country. In 1930 the first power from Ardnacrusha was fed into the network. Ireland had entered a new era in terms of the supply of energy.

There was no shortage of scoffers when the Shannon Scheme was being planned. They though the project far too grandiose for a small country: it would produce more power than Ireland could ever use. It is easy now to see how wrong they were. The demand for electricity has many times outstripped the capacity of the original Shannon Scheme. Additional hydro-electric stations have been built on the Lee, the Liffey, the Erne and the Clady; turf burning stations have been built on the bogs—the biggest at Ferbane, Rhode and Lanesboro; and a new oil-burning station at Ringsend, Dublin, right beside the old Pigeon House, will itself have ten times the capacity of the Shannon Scheme.

The great virtue of electricity is its mobility. The power lines can go more or less anywhere. Within the last generation the E.S.B.'s rural electrification scheme has brought a supply to every town and village and even into quite isolated homes. The individual farmer can now have a supply of light and power in his own yard. Industrially, electricity has reduced the competitive disadvantages of the remoter areas: a factory in Dingle or Gortahork can have

The laying of the trans-Atlantic cable from Valentia to Newfoundland: men on board the Great Eastern prepare for the final attempt to grapple the lost cable, 1865. (Illustrated London News).

its supply of power on the same terms as a competitor in Cork or Dublin. Moreover, since electricity came factories no longer have to be dirty. The factories of the coal age were ugly, and they spread ugliness all around them. Now a factory can be placed in the middle of a housing development without ruining life for the people who live there.

Electricity has a great deal to do with modern communications, too. Communication in its simplest form is word of mouth. The next simplest form is the letter: a written message which is carried from one man to another. Six generations ago, letters did not feature in an ordinary man's life at all. To begin with, he was probably unable to read or write; and in any case the post was quite expensive. In 1818 the cost of sending a letter from Dublin to Cork would be as much as a day's wages for a farm labourer. A letter to London cost twice as much. At these prices, the post was a luxury: the ordinary man never sent or received a letter in his entire life. Correspondence was confined to Government officials, businessmen and the well-to-do.

In 1840 Sir Rowland Hill introduced the penny post. For the price of a penny stamp a letter could travel to any part of these islands. The price of postage included delivery (there had been no local delivery previously except in Dublin). Now the letter-carrier—

forerunner of our postman—became a familiar figure everywhere. Correspondence became commonplace, especially as more and more people were learning to read and write. Pillar boxes were introduced to simplify the posting and collection of letters: some of those still in use were put up in the time of Queen Victoria—the period can be worked out from the letters or monogram on the box.

About the middle of the 19th century the railway revolutionised transport; and about the same time the electric telegraph created a revolution in communications. The principle of the telegraph is simple: electric impulses are transmitted over a wire, and are used as signals or codes to denote letters of the alphabet. The telegraph was revolutionary because it freed communications from the limitations of transport. When the French army landed at Killala in 1798, the Government in Dublin had no means of knowing about the invasion until a man on horseback galloped in with the news. But seventy years later, in the Fenian rising, the Government commandeered all the telegraph lines, and so they had instant information of every move made by the Fenian leaders.

The first submarine telegraph lines between Ireland and Britain were laid in the early 1850s. The next step was to establish a link with America, and this meant laying a cable 3,000 miles long on

Operators in the Telegraph House, Valentia, receiving messages from the Great Eastern, 1866. (Illustrated London News).

the bed of the Atlantic. Two attempts were made but were unsuccessful. In 1865 the greatest ship afloat, Brunel's *Great Eastern*, was commissioned for a third attempt. The 3,000 miles of cable were loaded aboard. Another ship laid a length of cable out to sea from the terminal point at Valentia, Co. Kerry: the *Great Eastern* took it aboard, spliced it to the cable she was carrying, and set off for Newfoundland, paying out the cable as she went. In mid-Atlantic, disaster struck: the cable broke, and the attempt had to be abandoned.

A year later the *Great Eastern* tried again, and this time she landed the end of the cable successfully ashore in Newfoundland. Finally she managed to raise from the sea bed the broken end of the first cable. The news of her success was flashed back by the wire to the cable station at Valentia, and from there by the complete cable to Newfoundland. So from the deck of a ship in mid-Atlantic, almost simultaneous communication had been effected between the two continents. As further cables were laid across the Atlantic, Waterville and Valentia became the European terminals for most of the telegraphic traffic between the Old World and the New.

Communication was carried a step further with the introduction of the telephone. Now the human voice itself could be projected along wires and a conversation could be held between people hundreds of miles apart. The telephone was introduced here about 1880, but development was slow: in fact Ireland is still relatively backward in the number and use of telephones. On the early telephone systems all connections were made manually through operators, but today telephone services all over the world are developing more and more towards fully automatic systems. Already a Dublin subscriber can dial a number in Limerick or Cork: soon probably he will be able to dial a number in London, Rome or Tokyo.

Both the telegraph and the telephone depend essentially on sending a signal along a wire. There was still a need for a more flexible system, in which wires between caller and receiver would not be necessary. This was especially desirable for communication between ships at sea, or from ship to shore. The new invention—called wireless telegraphy, or simply wireless—was devised by an Italian, Guglielmo Marconi. He established a company to exploit his invention and in 1900 he opened the first trans-Atlantic wireless cable station at Clifden. At the time the wireless telegraph was thought of principally as an aid to navigation, but Marconi's invention led directly to the whole complex of radio and television broadcasting that we know today.

These developments in communication have meant a great deal

Rehearsal in progress in RTE television studio.

in terms of news and public information. Six generations ago it took at least two or three days for news to travel from London to Dublin—much longer if ships were delayed by bad weather. News from abroad travelled at a similar speed. The Battle of Waterloo, fought on June 19, 1815, was reported in the Dublin papers of June 26, seven days later. But after the telegraph came into use, news could cross the Irish Sea in a flash. The great political debates at Westminster on the Irish Question, even if they ran on well after midnight, were all reported in the Dublin morning papers. At the same time the price of papers dropped sharply—down to a penny—and a lot more people were learning to read. The result was that, as the twentieth century came in, people were better informed than ever before about events in their own country and abroad.

Regular radio broadcasting, incorporating a news service, began in Ireland in 1926. Television was launched on December 31, 1961, and by 1970 nearly half a million homes around the country had television receivers. Irish people have joined with the people of Europe and the rest of the world in watching live pictures of such events as the moon-walk in July, 1969. Though these media of instant communication Ireland has become part of the "global village", and the Irishman of today has the opportunity to know more about the world than his grandfather or even his father ever did.

XIV: The Sources of Local History

History is usually regarded as the story of a nation. But the currents of change that are set off by great national or international events shape the lives of men and women in thousands of little communities as well as nations; and the story of these changes is history too. The evidence for local history is not confined to documents accessible only to a scholar. It can be read by an observant eye in the pattern of streets and roads, in the style of houses and castles, and in the condition of individual buildings. When a a community changes its habits it may abandon some buildings and leave them to decay; others may be adapted or rebuilt to serve a new function. So the physical remains in a town or village will throw light on its origins and early character and on its later development or decline.

Most Irish towns have certain features in common. First, medieval buildings may be still standing, usually in the form of a castle or a church. Substantial settlements were usually protected by a ring of walls; and the street pattern, growing up with this ring, will reflect its local purpose of serving life inside the walls, and will be less purposeful than the layout of a town which has emerged initially from building along the line of several converging roads. A careful examination of the street pattern in any town or village will provide clues as to its origins and functions.

Secondly, in the heart of most Irish towns the bulk of house-building took place between 1780 and 1830, and houses of this period still predominate. Thirdly, the growth of town populations slowed down by about 1830, but significant road developments occurred at that time on the fringes of the towns.

Fourthly, from about 1850 onwards for more than a century, remarkably few changes (apart from some road improvements) took place in most country towns. The main changes were the addition of institutional buildings—churches, schools, hospitals, railway stations and administrative buildings. Even where the Famine or the subsequent emigration affected a town severely, it was mainly the cabins on the approach roads that were abandoned; the poor still tended to crowd into the laneways of the central districts because of their convenience. In the last quarter of a century the process has been reversed, as families have been moved out into newly-developed housing estates on the outskirts, leaving the central lanes empty.

We can follow the growth of most Irish towns in the deeds registered in the Registry of Deeds since 1708. A fuller picture emerges from the first valuation of the 1830s; it lists the buildings in each town,

Galway: view up the Corrib from the Claddagh; Bartlett's sketch of c.1840. (National Library).

house by house, at the very time when the central districts had just taken on their final shape. Other documentary sources are scattered. Minutes of local bodies will throw some light on the administration of the towns but less on their social and economic life. Printed sources such as the *Journals of the House of Commons* (for the 18th century) or the Parliamentary Papers (for the 19th) will sometimes yield information. For manuscript sources, R. J. Hayes' *Guide to the Manuscript Sources for the History of Irish Civilisation* is a substantial but by no means complete index. Local newspapers—published since the 18th century in many Irish towns —can be helpful, though early copies have not always survived. Maps are very valuable: from the time of the first Ordnance Survey in the 19th century Ireland is well mapped, and the layout of towns and the pattern of settlement in the countryside are easy to visualise.

To put flesh on the bare bones one may look to topographical and historical writings. Lewis's *Topographical Dictionary of Ireland,* 1837, provides much detail on towns and villages. More specialised surveys may be found, such as Dutton's *Statistical Survey of County Clare,* 1808. Marmion's *Ancient and Modern History of the Maritime Ports of Ireland,* 1855, is very useful for port towns. Travellers' journals show the impression made by the district on an outsider. For instance, W. M. Thackeray, the English novelist, in his *Irish Sketch-Book*, makes some vivid comments on Ireland as he saw it before the Famine.

Some counties have been fortunate in that full accounts of them were compiled in the Ordnance Survey Memoirs. These were compiled mostly for the North. The *Ordnance Survey Memoir for the Parish of Antrim*, published by the Public Record Office of

FISH MARKET. GALWAY. 906. W.L.

The Corrib, looking downstream, c. 1900, showing a wooden bridge added since the scene in 1840 (see p.115). This wooden bridge has been replaced by a modern structure in the photograph on p.117. The last photograph reveals the disappearance of quay-side animation.

Northern Ireland, is a very full account of the topography, the economy and the social life of the town of Antrim at the end of the classic phase in the creation of modern Irish towns. For most towns, unfortunately, we cannot rely on contemporaries having put the information together for us: we have to piece the picture together from many sources. Guides to the use of material for local history are: T. P. O'Neill: *Sources of Irish Local History* (Library Association of Ireland, 1958); Public Record Office of Northern Ireland: *Sources for the Study of Local History in Northern Ireland*, 1968; J. Andrews: *Ireland in Maps* (Dolmen Press, 1961). The Public Record Office of Northern Ireland in Belfast has a series of leaflets on different categories of records—valuation records, local history searching, maps and plans—which, while intended for students in Northern Ireland, are useful also in directing students elsewhere towards the kind of material that may help their work.

County and diocesan histories are very relevant, and where a local historical or archaeological society exists its published proceedings represent, over the years, a valuable accumulation of knowledge of a region's history and guidance to the sources of it.

Personal or family reminiscences can often be of great value in giving us a picture of life in a particular district. Some of the best works available in this category are: Tomás O Criomhthain, *An*

116

t-Oileánach (The Blaskets); Peig Sayers, *Peig* (The Blaskets); Muiris O Súilleabháin, *Fiche bliain ag fás* (The Blaskets); M. MacGabhann, *Rotha Mór an tSaoil* (translated into English as *The Hard Road to Klondyke*) (Co. Donegal); Patrick Gallagher, *My Story, by Paddy the Cope* (Co. Donegal); M. Carbery, *The Farm by Lough Gur* (Co. Limerick); S. Andrews, *Nine Generations: a History of the Andrews Family, Millers of Comber* (Co. Down); E. de Blaghd, *Trasna na Bóinne* (Co. Antrim); R. McHugh, ed., *Carlow in '98*, first two chapters (Carlow town); W. Steuart Trench, *Realities of Irish Life* (Cos. Kerry and Monaghan); W. M. Scott, ed., *A Hundred Years a-Milling* (Co. Tyrone); Elizabeth Bowen, *The Bowens of Bowen's Court* (North Cork); J. M. Calwell, *Old Irish Life* (Co. Galway); Frank O'Connor, *An Only Child* (Cork city); Florence Mary McDowell, *Other Days Around Me* (Co. Antrim); Joseph Brady, *The Big Sycamore* (Co. Tipperary).The Irish poetry of the 17th, 18th or early 19th centuries may also illustrate aspects of the social life in a district at that time.

Illustrations are of great value in re-creating the past, but it is not easy to find pictures for the 18th century and earlier. Prints and engravings featured beautiful scenery and romantic ruins; those of towns often afford only a general prospect. For the town of Ennis there are virtually no pictures between Dineley's sketch of 1680 and a faded photograph of the inauguration of the O'Connell monument on the site of the old court house in 1867. Town centres were, in general, so completely rebuilt during the half-century or so after 1780 that it is difficult to visualise what they looked like

Galway: view up the Corrib from the Claddagh, 1970.

clopieur (nat.)

On the left, one of Harvey's sketches of Irish labourers about 1850;

when the older houses were still standing and there were green spaces around what is now the core of the town. From 1840 onwards, on the other hand, changes have not been all that numerous, and the similarities are as striking as the differences. Compare for instance the sketch of Galway, looking up the Corrib, made by Bartlett about 1840, with a photograph of the same location around 1900 and again in 1970.

Some of the older illustrations show us details of sociàl life sketched into larger subjects. Malton's prints of Dublin are primarily topographical, but the details in them give us interesting information on how people looked and what they did. In the print of St. Catherine's Church, for instance, there is a small group of women drawing water from a street fountain. But illustrations like these must be approached with a little caution. Artists in the 19th century

often had a romantic streak, and they had a tendency to represent any healthy country girl as a Dresden shepherdess. Compare the two sketches from the mid-19th century of an Irish rural labourer. The one on the left is a much more realistic portrayal than the other. At the other end of the scale, artists were sometimes influenced by the grotesque concept of the stage-Irishman; and this sometimes affected even the approach of those who were meant to be making realistic sketches for the *Illustrated London News*.

A teacher setting out to organise a project will find it easier in a town than in a rural district. A town is more compact; it has been the vital link between the outside world and its own hinterland; and so its significance is more obvious and its development is easier to trace. For either town or rural community, the first step is to survey the physical remains in the district, such as the ruins of a

119

castle or old mills. These will tell much of the story and will suggest lines of inquiry to be followed. Even where the physical remains have disappeared, an association may survive in a street name.

The students should then try to relate the growth of the area to some of the sources. Some of the printed sources are readily available; others are much harder to trace, but may prove very rewarding. Among the Parliamentary Papers, the enquiry into the poor in the 1830s has a mass of information on different rural districts; the enquiry into the housing of the labouring classes in 1885 is revealing on housing conditions in selected towns; and in the same year the committee appointed to enquire into Irish industries often refers, in its minutes of evidence, to industrial conditions in individual towns.

Old guidebooks, booklets prepared for local events or exhibitions, old photographs and postcards often survive and will throw light on local conditions. Even the tombstones in a local graveyard may have a tale to tell. In a town records may survive for the municipality, for a religious congregation, for the workhouse, for old-established and even for extinct businesses. The research done by teachers and students may bring such material to light and may be instrumental in saving it. Students should be encouraged to search out family papers—old property deeds, old accounts, say, or letters from relatives—and family photographs, and to care for their survival. Many a picture which seems commonplace now will be invaluable in years to come. It is precisely because old pictures and papers seemed commonplace to their custodians that so little survives throwing light on the ordinary conditions and the ordinary people of the past.

Members of the class may be asked, too, to go out and talk to older people about their memories of the old days. Local tradition can be accurate in many respects and very durable, and such recollections may provide unusual information about the district.

Town and countryside are inter-related. A rural district is usually part of the hinterland of a town, and its history should be related to that of the town and to the developments and changes in communications.

In all these studies students should be encouraged to become familiar with the local library and to draw, so far as is reasonable, on the expert knowledge of the librarian and his staff. But, most of all, they should be helped to develop the habit of close and accurate observation. They may not pursue their enquiry in depth, but they can greatly enrich their own lives by an understanding of the place in which they have their roots.